A Book of

Famous

Queens

By Lydia Farmer

Revised by Willard A. Heaps

THOMAS Y. CROWELL COMPANY
NEW YORK

Copyright © 1964 by Thomas Y. Crowell Company
All rights reserved. No part of this book may
be reproduced in any form, except by a reviewer,
without the permission of the publisher.
Designed by Ernst Reichl
Manufactured in the United States of America
by the Vail-Ballou Press, Inc., Binghamton, New York
Library of Congress Catalog Card No. 63-18413
First Printing

Preface

Throughout history many remarkable women stand out as rulers. From earliest times they have left their marks on their nations and times.

As early as fourteen centuries before Christ, we find such an outstanding figure as Nefertiti, who helped her husband build the splendid City of the Sun on the banks of the Nile. Later there was the beautiful Cleopatra, who captivated both Julius Caesar and Mark Antony, and all but overturned the Roman Empire. There were Zenobia, the heroic queen of Palmyra, and Isabella of Spain, best known as the patron of Christopher Columbus on his voyages of discovery to the New World, but quite as important for her other roles as law-maker and military leader.

Still others in this distinguished company are Catherine de' Medici of France, Queen Elizabeth of England, and Mary, Queen of Scots.

In the eighteenth century we have the great Maria Theresa of Austria and Catherine II of Russia as rulers, and Marie Antoinette and Josephine as wives of rulers.

Two nineteenth-century queens ruled for many years: Queen Victoria of England, whose reign of almost sixty-four years was longer than that of any other monarch in English history, and Tzu Hsi, empress dowager of China for almost half a century.

In more recent years, the influence of women is shown in the reigns of Wilhelmina of the Netherlands and her daughter, Juliana, admired for their wisdom, judgment, and simple democratic way of life.

Finally, there is Queen Elizabeth II of England, lacking many of the political powers of earlier queens, but completely dedicated to her country.

Here are famous queens who have made history. The impact of their lives for better or for worse upon peoples and events has been significant, and their stories form a fascinating study of feminine ambition, courage, intelligence, and self-sacrifice.

Contents

A Book of
Famous
Queens

Nefertiti

About 1390-1360 B.C.

Today Nefertiti is one of the most celebrated queens of ancient history, but for centuries
little was known of her, her husband Akhenaten, or
the splendid capital they built at Tell el 'Amarna on
the banks of the Nile in Egypt. Not long after Nefertiti's death, the city Akhetaten was abandoned.
As the years passed, the handsome limestone buildings so carefully erected by the pharaoh's workmen
fell into ruin. The palaces and temples, the royal
tombs, the customs house, and the people's homes
were slowly covered by the drifting sands which
blew in from the desert. Only the mighty river remained unchanged, while Akhetaten lay buried and
forgotten for three thousand years.

It was an Egyptian peasant woman who some
time in the 1880's reminded the world of what had
happened at Tell el 'Amarna. She left her village to
look for fuel and, crossing the sand dunes which
bordered the river, came unknowingly upon the site
of Akhetaten. Rummaging about, she unearthed
some clay objects which she recognized to be very
old and later tried to sell. By this time most Egyptians realized the value of artifacts and made a little
money now and then disposing of them to dealers
and museums. At first no one seemed to want the
pieces of clay, which were covered with scratches.
In their travels from museum to museum, some were
chipped and others were lost. Finally, however,
some were identified as letters written to Akhenaten's foreign office from neighboring kings request-
ing military help in time of war. Immediately archaeologists knew they had made an extremely exciting
discovery.

The deciphering of these letters marked the beginning of the reconstruction of the unusual story of
Akhenaten and Nefertiti. Ever since, archaeologists
from many parts of the world have been laboriously
matching the clues revealed by this and later finds.
Many questions about the royal couple and their life
still remain unanswered.

Exactly where and when Nefertiti was born is
not definitely known. It is believed that she married

Crown Prince Amenhotep IV at Thebes, then the capital of Egypt, when she was about eighteen. Her name meant "the beautiful lady comes," and all evidence points to the fact that the future queen was indeed lovely. Just before World War I a German archaeological expedition working at Tell el 'Amarna found a small sculptured head of Nefertiti which has since become world famous. Now in the Berlin Museum, it reveals a face with even, delicate features, high cheekbones, heavy-lidded eyes, and a full mouth.

Nefertiti had short, dark hair. Only a wisp showed at the back when she wore her tall, jeweled, helmet crown. Usually she dressed in white linen so finely woven that it shimmered like silk. Her robes were long and full, held in loosely at the waist by a golden belt studded with gems. One shoulder was bare, the other covered by her robe, which was held in place by a jeweled clasp. Bracelets adorned her upper arms, earrings sparkled in her ears, and her long, slim fingers were heavy with rings.

At the time of his marriage Amenhotep IV was twenty-one, an intelligent, sensitive, but unhealthy young man. He was presumably Nefertiti's brother or half-brother. Both are thought to have been children of Amenhotep III, then the pharaoh of Egypt. Such marriages were common within the reigning family. Amenhotep IV may have been influenced intellectually by his mother, Queen Tiy, who was a powerful figure in the court and had much to say about the government.

Amenhotep ruled jointly with his father until the pharaoh's death when he assumed full responsibility for the empire. He and Nefertiti lived in the royal palace which was surrounded by elaborate flower gardens and exotic trees imported from Asia. A lake was nearby and in the distance dark hills rose abruptly against the blue sky. Inside the palace the ceilings and walls were brilliantly painted with wild-life scenes—birds, flowers, fish, and animals. Here Nefertiti's first child was born, the first of seven daughters.

Nefertiti appears to have been treated as her husband's equal. He was devoted to her and in one tribute called her his "Great of Favor, Mistress of Happiness, at hearing whose Voice one rejoices, soothing the heart of the King at home, Great and Beloved Wife of the King." Paintings show them standing side by side, a remarkable change from the days when pharaohs were considered gods and all others were held in subservience and so portrayed in art. The two are also pictured holding hands or kissing, with children on their knees, and in natural, everyday attitudes. Amenhotep encouraged a close, informal family life.

The relationship between the pharaoh and the priests of the Egyptian religion, however, was not so pleasant. Amenhotep, who had a vigorous, questioning mind, was far ahead of his contemporaries in his ideas, which Nefertiti shared. Both believed in one universal god, Aten, the god of the sun, while the religion of the time centered upon the worship of many gods. The priests, with their established religious conventions, were fearful of the young pharaoh and his new concepts, particularly since he had the power to silence them. As Amenhotep grew more outspoken and his relations with the priesthood became more strained, he began to dream of founding a new capital city on land never before dedicated to any god. He planned to call it Akhetaten or "the Horizon of the Disk" in honor of Aten, and he took the sun's disk as his symbol. This symbol, with each of the sun's descending rays ending in a hand, appears with him in the paintings of the period.

With some of his supporters Amenhotep sailed northward on the Nile, searching for the perfect site on which to build the city of his dreams. He found it at Tell el 'Amarna, nearly two hundred miles from Thebes, at a bend in the river where a wide, sandy plain stretched back to protecting limestone cliffs. Here he ordered his men to begin work. After some months there rose a palace for the royal family, a temple for worship, homes for the nobles, stables, granaries, and wharves for the royal fleet, as well as for trading ships.

In Thebes, Nefertiti, who by now had three daughters, readied her family for the long trip. Then the court and its followers set sail. After several days they dropped anchor at Akhetaten, where the new buildings were ready for occupancy and flowers were blooming in what had been sandy wastes. At the dedication of the city, the pharaoh changed his own name to honor his god. From then on he was called Akhenaten, meaning "it is well with Aten."

Nefertiti usually accompanied her husband on his business around the capital. In their chariot drawn by prancing horses they drove over the paved streets to visit the glassworks, the alabaster quarries, and the marketplace. Sometimes they took their children to the palace zoo where there were lions, panthers, lynxes, and ocelots. At the balcony of audience they listened to the petitions of their subjects. Rich and poor alike were permitted to come there to ask favors of the pharaoh and his queen.

Nefertiti had other duties, too. She attended several religious ceremonies each day, usually at sunrise and sunset. Akhenaten was zealous in his dedication to the new religion and determined to wipe out all traces of the old. To him Aten was the source of all life, the power which created all things. He was also a god of love, in contrast to the earlier gods, who were often harsh and vengeful. He could be found in nature, in the beauty of the flowers and the trees. It is recorded that Aten caused the "birds to flutter in the marshes and the sheep to dance upon their feet," so concerned was he with the simplest living things. The emphasis of the religion was on beauty, love, and truth. We do not know where Akhenaten got these ideas, which were astonishing for one who lived almost 1400 years previous to the time that Christ spoke of a similar creator of life and benevolent father.

Nefertiti's and Akhenaten's religion appears to have included little ceremony. There were no idols, and the few sacrifices offered by the priests were usually fruits and flowers. Psalms were sung and one of the most beautiful was a hymn to Aten written by Akhenaten himself. The children participated in these services and were instructed early in their parents' code of ethics.

Like other Eygptian wives Nefertiti often went to school with her children. Priests conducted the classes in the temples. They taught the alphabet, the zodiac, the calendar, the telling of time by water clocks, writing, mathematics, geometry, and astronomy. In the higher grades students were permitted to use paper made from the papyrus plant. The stem of the plant was cut into strips, other strips were placed crosswise on these, and the sheet was pressed. The paper was so strong that records from Nefertiti's time are still legible.

Nefertiti was interested in encouraging the cultural life of the city. She urged her husband to invite artists, sculptors, architects, poets, philosophers, musicians and other talented men to the court. Akhenaten himself wrote poetry. He was also responsible for the marked change in art style during his reign. The representations of the human figure became much more realistic and the poses less stylized and more natural. The pharaoh insisted that artists draw or paint him as he was, and so we find Akhenaten shown with his long, narrow head, sharp chin, and protruding stomach. The rules which had dominated thousands of years of Egyptian art were rejected, and the artist was encouraged to paint honestly what he saw.

Also unconventional was the attitude toward women. They enjoyed a great deal of freedom. They walked in the streets unattended and unharmed, engaged in industry and trade, held and willed property in their own names, and contributed much to the administration of civic affairs. The husband made over his property and future earnings to his wife in the marriage settlement. Girls, as well as boys, were reared and educated with care.

Sometimes, when the duties of the day were over, Akhenaten and Nefertiti gave large parties. We can imagine one such occasion when they may have awaited the arrival of their guests in the portico of the summer palace. The queen was dressed, as usual, in a loose white robe and was adorned with her jewels. The king wore an opaque white kilt which fell to his knees. Over it was thrown a tunic of soft white wool. He, too, wore bracelets, earrings, rings, and gold anklets set with precious stones.

As Nefertiti glanced over the gardens to the river beyond, she could see the guests arriving. Some came by boat, singing as they approached, some by horse-drawn chariot, and a few who lived nearby were on foot. Beside Nefertiti, a handmaiden stood ready with a huge basket of mauve-tipped lotus blossoms, one of which the queen presented to each female visitor as she greeted her.

Soon the great inner room, its walls painted with flying birds and flowers, was crowded with people. Under a deep blue ceiling, painted to represent the night sky resplendent with stars, the guests sipped delicate wines in crystal goblets.

The banquet which followed offered lentil soup, roast beef, lamb, goose, wild fowl, bread made from the papyrus and the lotus, cheeses, olives, the eggs of wild birds, and huge platters of fish from the Nile.

Gold and silver bowls were heaped high with figs, dates, pomegranates, tangerines, grapes, and bananas.

Later the party moved to the music room, a huge hall splendid with tapestries, rugs, and bright-colored cushions. The tables were gay with flowers and fruit, and more wine was brought in by the serving maids. Then the guests sat back to listen to the lutes, the harps, and the muted drums. Later still the gathering was entertained by tumblers, dancing boys, and jesters. It was early in the morning before the guests departed. Nefertiti and Akhenaten lingered in the gardens after bidding farewell to their friends. Hand in hand they stood in the moonlight, perhaps silently thanking Aten for their peaceful city on the Nile.

Unfortunately, life was not always to be free from sorrow. The first tragedy came when Maketaten, their second daughter, died. She was about nine years old. Akhenaten was inconsolable, for she had been his favorite child. She was buried with traditional ceremonies in the royal tomb. Her furniture, toys, and other personal possessions were placed with her, as was the custom, and gold, silver, and precious stones were piled around them. Then masons bricked up the opening and it was secured with plaster seals.

Nefertiti was saddened by the loss of her child,

but as time passed she was even more grieved at the change in her husband. Always a shy, introspective man, he now spent more and more time alone. Some sort of rift seems to have developed between Akhenaten and Nefertiti. Possibly it was a difference in belief, for there is evidence that Akhenaten might have begun to make his peace with the priests in Thebes, while Nefertiti remained an ardent Atenist. It is known that Queen Tiy came from Thebes to visit her son in the twelfth year of his reign, and she may have acted as a peacemaker between the two cities. Three years after her visit Akhenaten arranged the marriage of his daughter Meritaten to his half brother Smenkhkare and made him coregent. Smenkhkare went back to Thebes with his wife and ruled from there, possibly to placate the rebellious subjects. Smenkhkare looks very much like Akhenaten in his pictures and Meritaten has the long head and alert face of her mother.

Nefertiti appears to have withdrawn to another palace, taking ten-year-old Tutankhaten, another half brother of Akhenaten's, with her. The lonely Akhenaten then married his own daughter, Ankhsenpaaten. Several years later he died on his throne and was buried in the tomb where his daughter Maketaten lay. His reign had lasted seventeen years. On one of the walls of the tomb, cut into the plaster, archaeologists later found the figures of Akhenaten,

Nefertiti, and the princesses, their hands held out toward the familiar sun disk in blessing.

As far as we can tell, Nefertiti lived on in her palace for a few more years. She arranged the marriage of the boy Tutankhaten to her daughter, Ankhsenpaaten, Akhenaten's widow. Since Tutankhaten was still a child, Nefertiti held the actual power.

No one knows where or when Nefertiti died. Nor has her place of burial ever been found. Possibly the revolutionary ideas cultivated by Nefertiti and Akhenaten lived on in the minds of a few loyal followers. For most, however, the era of Atenism came to an end. Tutankhaten and his wife moved to Thebes and embraced the old religion that Akhenaten had rejected. Tutankhaten took the name by which we know him—Tutankhamen—to mark the change. The priests returned to power. They saw that all references to Akhenaten and Nefertiti were removed from the monuments and paintings and that the temples to Aten were destroyed. The city of Akhetaten was gradually abandoned until, only twenty-five years after its building, it was empty of human life.

Cleopatra

69-30 B.C.

The name Cleopatra, queen of Egypt, immediately suggests a capricious siren who held the two greatest men of her day under her spell. In this popular conception she has been much maligned, because such oversimplification of her character fails to consider the qualities of mind which made her attractive to both Julius Caesar and Mark Antony, the two great loves in her short life. Furthermore, she was an ambitious politician who was eager to advance the fortunes of her country through association with Rome. Those who regard her only as a shallow courtesan underestimate one of the most remarkable and colorful queens in all world history.

Cleopatra, the seventh Egyptian queen of her

name, was born just before the Christian era, in the winter of 69–68 B.C. Though by birth she was an Egyptian, by ancestry she was a Greek. Her Macedonian forebears were descended from one of the generals of Alexander the Great. He had conquered Egypt and established the ruling line of the Ptolemies. The early kings of this line were distinguished for wise government and the advancement of their people in arts, sciences, and literature, and Alexandria was developed into a cultural center by them. But succeeding Ptolemies grew more and more vicious, weak, and sensual. The great-grandfather of Cleopatra stands forth in history as a hideous example of vice and crime.

Ptolemy XIII, Cleopatra's father, was a murderous and treacherous alcoholic. When he died, his will directed that the throne of Egypt was to be held by eighteen-year-old Cleopatra and her younger brother, eleven-year-old Ptolemy, who were to marry each other and reign jointly. Such a marriage of convenience, to retain royal powers within a family, was customary among Egyptian monarchs. Cleopatra and Ptolemy XIV reigned in name only, the government being conducted by two ministers, the eunuch Potheinus and the general Achillas.

In 48 B.C. these two ambitious men deposed Cleopatra and placed her brother alone on the throne. They did not trust the quick-witted and resourceful queen, who was now twenty-one, but believed they could readily manage her brother, who was only fourteen years old.

They soon realized, however, that they could not so easily dispose of Cleopatra, who fled to Syria to raise troops to fight for her rightful inheritance. She obtained an army and began her march back into Egypt. Potheinus and Achillas, with a large body of soldiers, went forth to meet her. The two armies encamped near Pelusium, near modern Port Said. But no battle was fought, owing to unexpected circumstances.

Julius Caesar, the brilliant Roman military leader, was in pursuit of Pompey, his defeated rival for control of the Roman Empire, and had reached Pelusium with his small force. Since Pompey had once given financial aid to Cleopatra's father, he fled to Egypt in the hope of finding asylum there. But he was treacherously invited by the two Egyptian ministers to land in a deserted spot and was murdered while stepping ashore.

Julius Caesar then arrived at Alexandria in pursuit of Pompey. When Potheinus and Achillas heard he was there, they and King Ptolemy quickly returned to the city. Hoping to win Caesar's favor, they sent him the head of the murdered Pompey. But, far from being pleased, Caesar was deeply shocked. He learned of the intrigues and plots of the two ministers and decided to remain in Alexandria and aid Cleopatra, who was still in exile, to regain her throne.

Caesar secretly sent orders to her to return to Alexandria. Accordingly she took a small boat with only one attendant and landed at dusk near the palace. But she did not know how to get into it without being seen and captured. Then she hit upon the idea of having her servant roll her up in a bundle of blankets. He tied it so that it looked like a bale of merchandise, lifted it over his shoulder, and carried it to the palace gates.

When the guards questioned him, he replied that he carried a gift for Caesar. In this way he gained access to the Roman's apartment, and when the mysterious bundle was unrolled, even the stern general was captivated by what he saw and was immediately under her spell.

At this time the Egyptian queen was about twenty-one years of age. She was slender and graceful, and renowned not so much for her classic beauty as for her personal charm. As she pleaded her cause with lively intelligence and quick wit, Julius Caesar was completely bewitched. He who had conquered most of the known world was won over by this strong-minded, starry-eyed beauty of the Nile, and, though fifty-two, was soon like a lovesick boy.

Caesar took up Cleopatra's support with great fervor. He sent for the young king, Ptolemy XIV, and urged him to restore Cleopatra to her rights as joint sovereign in accordance with their father's wishes. But Ptolemy was angered that his sister had delivered herself into the power of a Roman. He left in a rage, tearing the crown from his head and shouting to the people that he had been betrayed.

The populace became so aroused by the claims of Ptolemy and his ministers, who told them that Caesar had seized and imprisoned Cleopatra, that they rushed to attack the palace. Caesar boldly sent out a small detachment of his soldiers, with orders to capture Ptolemy and bring him back as prisoner. This was speedily accomplished. Then Caesar addressed the angry mob on the street below his tower window, and assured them that, as a neutral mediator, he would endeavor to arbitrate the dispute between Cleopatra and her brother. Impressed by the words of the great Julius Caesar, the mob dispersed.

The next day Caesar convened an assembly of the chief men of Alexandria, and the decision was reached to restore Cleopatra to her rightful position as coruler with her brother. There seemed to be no open opposition to the settlement, and a festival was held to celebrate the reconciliation. However, during the feast one of Caesar's servants overheard and reported to him a plot by the Egyptian ministers, Potheinus and Achillas, to kill Caesar. Caesar thereupon had Potheinus put to death, but Achillas fled to join the Egyptian army, of which he was commander, and marched against Caesar.

The war which followed is known as the Alexandrine War. Achillas at first had the advantage, as his army was large and Caesar's reinforcements had not yet arrived. However, as a master of strategy, the Roman commander realized the importance of controlling all the approaches to the city. He therefore sent out an expedition to burn the shipping in the harbor and to take possession of a fort upon the island of Pharos, which commanded the entrance to the port. This undertaking was successful, but its accomplishment resulted in the burning of the famous Alexandria library, an irretrievable loss to the entire world.

The Egyptians were finally defeated, and the victorious Caesar placed Cleopatra again on the throne of Egypt. Her brother and nominal husband, Ptolemy, had been killed in the war, but a younger brother of the same name was given equal rights to the throne.

Caesar tarried in Egypt for two years. He was so infatuated with Cleopatra that, although he was already married to a Roman lady, Calpurnia, he took the lovely queen of Egypt as a wife. Under the Egyptian concept of the divinity of their rulers, Caesar was considered as a god (Amen reappeared in the flesh) even as their queen was a goddess. The two shared the dream of becoming monarchs of a combined Egypto-Roman empire. Their son, born in 47 B.C. and named Caesarion (little Caesar), was to be their joint heir, or at least Cleopatra's successor to the throne of Egypt.

But the affairs of the Roman Empire called Caesar, and he returned to Rome by way of Syria, where he put down a rebellion. After further successful campaigning in North Africa, he was welcomed in his capital with a magnificent celebration.

With her year-old son and her young brother Ptolemy XV, Cleopatra joined Caesar in Rome for his triumph. Her arrival there, where Calpurnia lived, naturally caused a scandal which was intensified by Caesar's construction of a temple to Venus, goddess of love, with a statue of Cleopatra in the place of honor. Two years later Julius Caesar met his death at the hands of conspirators on the ides of March, 44 B.C. His funeral oration was delivered by Mark Antony, who was to follow him in Cleopatra's affection.

Caesar's will named his grandnephew, nineteen-year-old Octavian, as his heir. To protect her own interests, Cleopatra asked both Cicero and Mark Antony to consider the rights of little Caesarion, but was unsuccessful. Fearing that her own life was in danger—for the Roman people were much incensed against her because of her influence over Caesar—

she fled secretly to Egypt with her son. Her younger brother, Ptolemy XV, died in Rome. Some have said that he was poisoned by Cleopatra so that she might reign as sole monarch, but the evidence is inconclusive. Caesarion was thus the uncrowned king of Egypt.

Octavian Caesar, Mark Antony, and Lepidus, a general, now formed the celebrated Roman triumvirate, and divided the Roman Empire among themselves. The battle of Philippi in 42 B.C., in which Brutus and Cassius were defeated, established the ascendancy of Antony, and made him the most influential man since Julius Caesar.

After her return to Egypt Cleopatra did not openly declare herself a partisan of either Mark Antony's friends or his enemies. But Antony was suspicious of her allegiance to Rome and sent an officer to summon the famous queen of the Nile to Tarsus to discuss the situation. Since he had become the most powerful man in the world, Cleopatra decided to go with as much pomp and magnificence as possible.

When Cleopatra's fleet sailed up the river Cydnus toward Tarsus, the sweet sounds of flutes, lyres, and cymbals preceded the ships. The citizens gathered along the banks, eager to catch the first glimpse of the source of such unusual music.

Then, from round the bend of the river glided a

gorgeous barge, its deck of beaten gold, its silken
sails of royal purple swelling in the light breeze.
Under a canopy of gold cloth a woman dressed as
Venus reclined upon a jeweled couch. She was surrounded by small boys dressed as Cupids, who
fanned her with ostrich plumes, and by lovely young
girls costumed as mermaids. Other maidens played
flutes and lyres. Clouds of incense wafted their per-
fume to the shore.

Antony had seated himself on a throne in the
marketplace, waiting for Cleopatra to land and pay
her respects to him. Instead, she ordered her tents
pitched. When she did not appear, Antony sent a
politely worded invitation asking her to dine with
him, but she replied that it would be more pleasing
to her to receive him and his officers as her guests.

When Antony and his generals entered her tents,
their magnificence astonished and bewildered him.
The dinner service was of gold set with precious
jewels, and the seats for the guests were ornamented
with purple and gold. Antony praised the splendor
all about him, and Cleopatra replied that these were
just trifles. If he found the service and the ornaments
pleasing, she begged that he accept them as a slight
gift from her. The next day Cleopatra was invited to
dine with Mark Antony, but though he tried to equal
the splendor of her entertainments, he fell so far

short that he ruefully acknowledged his defeat. Again and again, Antony and his generals were feted by Cleopatra.

The queen of Egypt was then twenty-five years of age, and her Oriental-Greek beauty was at its height. Her mind was mature and her wit unequaled. Her changing moods captivated Antony, and he found her altogether irresistible.

One evening at dinner when Antony playfully reproached her for her extravagance, she declared that dinner the next day should surpass all that had gone before and would cost ten thousand sestertia (equal to $300,000). Antony would not believe this and made a wager with her that she could not fulfill her promise.

When he arrived next day, he noticed no added magnificence and laughingly declared that she had lost the wager. "You shall see, my dear Antony," she replied. "I myself will soon eat and drink the ten thousand sestertia." Thereupon she removed from her ears two pearls, the largest in the world at that time. (At today's value they would be worth $222,-000 each.)

At her bidding a servant set before her a glass of vinegar. She dropped one of the pearls into the liquid, and when the pearl was dissolved, she drank the brew. She was about to sacrifice the other pearl when one of the generals snatched it from her, saying she had already won the wager. The rescued pearl was later taken to Rome and there cut in two and made into a pair of earrings for the statue of Venus in the Pantheon.

Cleopatra's charm made Antony forget Fulvia, his own wife, whom he had left in Rome, and also his duty to his country. He followed Cleopatra to Alexandria and there gave himself up to amusement and pleasure. The young queen employed every artifice to amuse her guest. She played dice with him, hunted by his side, was present at his military parades, and joined him in his night revels.

Yet her youth and beauty could not hide her innate cruelty. Her first request of Antony was for the death of her sister, Arsinoë, who had been living in exile in Cyprus. Cleopatra wanted her put out of the way because she was reported to be scheming to oust her. Accordingly Antony arranged Arsinoë's murder.

Next, Antony presented to her the large library of Pergamum, which had been part of his share in the spoils of war. Cleopatra placed the 200,000 books from Pergamum in the temple of Serapis, and once again Alexandria held the largest library in the world. These royal gifts caused the Romans to resent Antony bitterly and to hate even more the crafty Cleopatra whom they blamed for her evil influence over their general.

In 40 B.C. Antony undertook an expedition in Asia

Minor and while there he learned that his wife had died. When he had been absent from Alexandria only six months, Cleopatra gave birth to twins, a boy and a girl, whom she named Alexander Helios (the Sun) and Cleopatra Selene (the Moon). She did not see Antony again for more than three years.

Meanwhile, to strengthen his relations with the triumvirate, Antony married Octavia, the sister of Octavian. He appeared to have temporarily deserted Cleopatra, for within three years Octavia gave birth to two daughters. But when he left Rome on an expedition to Syria late in 37 B.C., he summoned Cleopatra to meet him. Because she feared that she was losing him, she demanded, when they met in Antioch, that their alliance be made a part of a binding contract. He gave her outright several of the provinces of the Roman Empire and publicly acknowledged his two children by her. He married her according to Egyptian law and recognized Caesarion, Cleopatra's son by Julius Caesar, as the rightful heir to the throne of Egypt. In return Cleopatra agreed to give Antony financial and military help whenever he should need them. When she returned to Alexandria she gave birth to a son, whom she named, according to custom, Ptolemy.

Mark Antony met one of his few humiliating defeats in Parthia in the year 36 B.C., then joined Cleopatra in Alexandria. For four years he enjoyed life there, becoming lazy and dissolute. Cleopatra's influence over him increased steadily. But when the term of the triumvirate expired in 32 B.C., Octavian did not wish to renew it. This was tantamount to a declaration of war. To make the breach even wider, Antony ordered his wife Octavia from his house in Rome with her children. Octavian was eager to avenge his sister.

Antony gathered together a large army and Cleopatra furnished troops and ships. They proceeded to Ephesus and then to Samos where, despite their impending peril, the royal couple passed many days in feasting and entertainment. It was during one of the feasts that Antony began to fear that in some moment of anger or treachery Cleopatra might poison him. He ordered that a servant taste first all the food served him. Cleopatra, realizing his mistrust, determined to teach him how completely he was in her power if she chose to harm him.

She therefore poisoned the stems of the flowers in the wreaths she and Antony wore at the table according to Egyptian custom. At their next feast she suggested that they pick some flowers from their crowns and drink them in their wine. Antony readily consented, and breaking off a few blossoms, he tossed them into his glass and raised it to his lips to drink. But Cleopatra quickly seized his uplifted arm and exclaimed, "I am the poisoner against whom you take such mighty precautions. If it were possible for me to live without you, judge now whether I wanted either opportunity or reason for such action." Then she commanded that a condemned prisoner drink the contents of Antony's glass. After doing so the prisoner fell dead at their feet.

At length Antony and Cleopatra were prepared and set forth with their combined fleet to meet their Roman foes. This fleet numbered five hundred great ships of war, but they were poorly manned. Octavian Caesar had only two hundred and fifty ships, but his war galleys were manned by experienced seamen and his troops were veterans of many wars. On the advice of Cleopatra, Antony decided to risk all in a naval battle rather than in conflict on land.

The battle was fought at Actium, off the coast of Greece, in 31 B.C., and has been adjudged by historians to be one of the most important and decisive of ancient times. In the midst of the conflict, when Antony's chances of success appeared to be favorable, Cleopatra became panic-stricken and ordered her sixty ships to leave.

During a lull in the battle Antony saw what had happened, and he transferred from his command galley to a smaller fast-sailing ship and hastened after her. Though the fleet, deserted by its commander, continued to fight heroically, Octavian finally gained the victory.

When Cleopatra saw that Antony was following her, she commanded her admiral to stop her galley and take Antony aboard. So great was his mortification and remorse, however, that he would not see or speak to her for three days. He must have felt keenly the humiliation of being so completely under the domination of a woman.

When they had returned to Alexandria, Antony was melancholy and dispirited, and his gloom increased when he received word that all his troops in all the dominions had surrendered to Octavian, and that nothing now remained to him save Egypt. Unable to bear Cleopatra's scorn, he moved from the palace and lived in solitude.

But Cleopatra knew that Octavian would invade Egypt as soon as he could rebuild his fleet and his legions. She now ordered that her ships be carried from the Mediterranean thirty miles over the desert isthmus into the Red Sea, so that they would be beyond the reach of any attack. But when the Arabians burned several of her ships she abandoned the plan.

Now followed a time of despair for Cleopatra. According to custom she had built a costly tomb for herself adjoining the temple of Isis. To this mausoleum she now brought her most precious treasures, including gold, silver, jewels, ebony, ivory, and many jars of perfumes. She also ordered an immense quantity of flax, tallow, and torches for use in case she should determine to destroy herself and her riches by fire.

When Octavian arrived at Alexandria in July of 30 B.C., Antony had prepared a good defense, for he had roused himself from his depression and become his old self. From a hilltop near the harbor, he watched the galleys which were to make the first attack on the approaching enemy fleet. Instead they saluted Octavian's ships with their oars, the sign of friendship. This treason opened Antony's eyes to the perfidy of his queen, but he was even more horrified when his cavalry galloped over to the lines of the enemy.

With one last impulse of his warlike valor, Antony challenged Octavian to single combat, but the latter laughed at him and replied that if Antony were weary of life there were other ways to die. Finding himself thus ridiculed by Caesar and betrayed by Cleopatra, Antony rushed in anger to the palace to avenge himself on the woman for whom he had bartered fatherland and honor.

Cleopatra, however, had retired into her tomb with two women attendants, and sent word to Antony that she had killed herself. When he heard the news, he thrust his sword into his side, but the wound was not immediately fatal. An officer soon arrived to tell him that Cleopatra was not dead, and the dying Antony opened his eyes and begged to be taken to her. Cleopatra would not allow her doors to be opened for fear her enemies would surprise her, so Antony was lifted through her window by ropes and died in her arms.

Octavian allowed Cleopatra to bury Antony with royal honors and afterward went to visit her. Her eyes were swollen with tears, her hair was loose and disordered, her face haggard with grief. Octavian assured her that she would be treated with kindness. But the queen knew that her kingdom was lost and that she would probably undergo the humiliation of being taken to Rome and displayed as a prisoner.

After Octavian had left her, Cleopatra dressed in her royal robes and put on her most dazzling jewels and her crown, dismissing all except two faithful women servants. She wrote a letter to Octavian and then asked for a basket of figs which a servant had brought her.

After Cleopatra had examined the figs, she lay down upon her couch, and soon afterward appeared to have fallen asleep. But an asp had been hidden, at her bidding, among the figs, and had stung her upon the arm. The poison reached her heart and killed her almost instantly.

When Octavian received her letter, in which she requested that she be buried beside Mark Antony, he sent officers quickly to her tomb. They found Cleopatra upon her bed of gold. One of her servants lay dead at her feet. The other attendant was adjusting the crown upon the brow of her mistress.

Seeing this, one of the Roman soldiers angrily exclaimed, "Is it right and fair that your queen should do this to us?"

"Very right," she replied, "and fitting for a princess descended from so many noble kings," and she fell dead.

Cleopatra was buried in royal state beside Antony. She was thirty-nine at the time of her death, and had reigned twenty-two stormy years. She was the last of her line, for after her death Egypt was reduced to a province of the Roman Empire. The reign of the Ptolemies had been uninterrupted for 293 years.

Caesarion, son of Cleopatra and Julius Caesar, was put to death by Octavian, but Cleopatra's younger children were taken to Rome and cared for by Antony's widow, Octavia.

Thus perished the famous Cleopatra whose life, played out on the stage of politics and war, encompassed contrasts of great happiness and despairing grief. Her beauty, fascination, and extravagance can be matched only in the tales of the Arabian Nights. Yet her ambition and the two fatal loves of her life doomed her to unhappiness and, finally, when all her glory was gone, to suicide.

3

Zenobia

Ruled A.D. 267-272

A present-day traveler through the desert country in the central part of Syria northeast of Damascus might possibly stop at a small Bedouin village named Tadmor. On this spot archaeologists have excavated the extensive remains of Palmyra, once a flourishing city. Long colonnades stretch over the desert wastes (375 columns may be counted, with 150 still standing upright), and ruins of an extensive marketplace and parts of a colossal pillared temple of Baal give some indication of what the spot might have been in the days of its glory more than seventeen centuries ago.

Like a green island rising unexpectedly in bleak mid-ocean, the Palmyra of that time cheered the sight of the tired traveler who had made his way over the wastes of the Syrian desert. This oasis with its groves of waving palm trees, first named Tadmor, was said to have been founded by Solomon as a resting place for caravans in the middle of the desert sands. Tadmor is mentioned in the Old Testament (II Chronicles 8:4). The name Palmyra was given to it by the Greeks.

Palmyra owed its importance to its strategic position at the junction of the main caravan routes between the Mediterranean ports of Syria and the Euphrates River as well as those connecting Arabia with Syria and Mesopotamia.

At the height of Palmyra's power even Rome paid it homage, and Roman emperors thought it not beneath them to seek alliance with its rulers. Flanked by high hills on the east, the city filled the plain below, both north and south, as far as the eye could reach. In its center was the vast temple of Baal with a thousand Ionic columns of dazzling white marble. The temple was a superb blending of varied types of architecture; around the central portion of the building rose pyramids, obelisks, domes, arches, and towers.

The marketplace was a long building flanked on both sides with rows of Corinthian columns. Here merchants assembled, exhibiting wares gathered from all parts of the known world; the camels and dromedaries of their caravans were herded nearby.

The Palmyrans were Egyptian in their origin and customs, Persian in their luxurious tastes, Grecian in their language, literature, and architecture.

Before this period of its grandeur, the growing city had been attacked by Mark Antony in 41 B.C., but the citizens had been forewarned and moved their possessions across the Euphrates River so that when his cavalry arrived the city was deserted. Later the Romans occupied it for many years.

When the Persians invaded the eastern Roman Empire in the middle of the third century after the birth of Christ, the king of Palmyra was Odenathus. His second wife, Zenobia, claimed descent from the Macedonian kings of Egypt. She equaled her famous ancestress Cleopatra in beauty and far surpassed her in virtues. We do not know whether she was Syrian, Arabian, Hebrew, or Egyptian.

She was a woman of rare intellectual powers, well versed in Latin, Greek, Syriac, and the Egyptian languages. The celebrated philosopher Longinus was her instructor, brought from Rome by Odenathus so that his queen would be worthy of her high position. The works of Homer and Plato were familiar to her, and she wrote with ease in Greek. She even compiled an Oriental history for her own use.

Zenobia's beauty was stunning. Her hair was glossy black, her complexion dark, her teeth pearly white, and her radiant eyes large and black. She possessed great strength and endurance, and often appeared on horseback. She usually accompanied her husband at the head of his troops.

Odenathus, strong, intelligent, and courageous, was chief of several desert tribes. He was so powerful that the Romans made him their ally and gave him the title of Augustus and General of the East, with the administration of the entire region between Egypt and Asia Minor. He repelled an invasion by Shapur, the king of Persia, twice pursuing his troops to the very gates of the capital. After these victories he called himself the King of Kings, yet he was still a Roman subject and the highest Roman official in the Near East.

But in the midst of his triumphs Odenathus was assassinated at Emesa while hunting. His murderer was his nephew, Maconius. Zenobia revenged the death of her husband by killing his slayer. Since her three sons were too young to rule, she first exercised power as queen regent. Later, in A.D. 267, she declared herself queen.

Zenobia was remarkable for her courage, prudence, and fortitude. No danger unnerved her, no fatigue dismayed her. From the first she governed her realm with sound judgment. If it was expedient to punish, she could act with manlike stoicism. If, on the other hand, it was justice to pardon, she could display magnanimous forgiveness.

Though on state occasions she clothed herself and her court with regal magnificence, so strict was her economy in government affairs that she was often accused of penury. But she spent immense sums for the beautification of Palmyra, and gathered around her philosophers, poets, and artists from many lands.

Gallienus, emperor of Rome, refused to acknowledge Zenobia's claim to the sovereignty of her husband's lands and twice sent an army against her, but was each time defeated. Her lands extended from the Euphrates to the Mediterranean, and included Jerusalem, Antioch, Damascus, and other cities famed in history. Zenobia, however, chose Palmyra as her place of residence and made expeditions from time to time to her other provinces.

In 270 Zenobia conquered Egypt and assumed the title queen of the East. Arabia, Armenia, and Persia became her allies. Her long-term objective was to achieve independence from Rome and establish Palmyra's rule over the entire Orient. She accordingly began to defer no longer to her Roman peers.

When Aurelian became emperor of Rome in 270, he was highly indignant that a woman should act so independently and defy Rome's power. Zenobia had challenged Rome and must be punished. After he had subdued all his competitors in the West, he turned his arms against this powerful queen of the East, who dared to call herself Augusta. This was in 271. Confident of his success, the emperor advanced across Asia Minor toward Palmyra.

When the first herald arrived to announce the Roman ambassadors who had been sent by Aurelian to demand her submission, Zenobia was at her hunting lodge just outside the city. The queen had just returned from the hunt and was mounted upon a white Arabian horse, its harness studded with jewels. Not waiting to dismount, she exclaimed, "Bid the servants of your emperor draw near, and we will hear them."

Announced by trumpets, the ambassadors advanced to the spot where Zenobia was calmly awaiting them. "Speak your errand," said the queen.

"For many years," replied Aurelian's spokesman, "the wealth of Egypt and the East flowed into the Roman treasury. That stream has been diverted to Palmyra. Egypt, Syria, Bithynia, and Mesopotamia were dependent upon Rome, as Roman provinces. The queen of Palmyra was once but the queen of Palmyra; she is now queen of Egypt and of the East. . . . By whatever consent of former emperors these honors have been won or permitted, it is not, we are required to say, with the consent of Aurelian. While he respects the greatness and genius of

Zenobia, he holds essential to his honor and the glory of the Roman world that the Roman Empire should again be restored to the limits which bounded it in the reigns of his predecessors."

"You have spoken," replied Zenobia, "with directness, as it becomes a Roman to do." Then she continued firmly: "Now hear me, and as you hear, so report to him who sent you. Tell Aurelian that I am what I am. I have made myself. The empire which hails me queen has been molded into what it is by Odenathus and Zenobia. It is no gift, but an inheritance, a conquest, a possession. It is held not by favor but by right of birth and power. When your master will give away possessions or provinces which he claims as his or Rome's, for the asking, I will give away Egypt and the Mediterranean coast. Tell him that as I have lived a queen, so, the gods helping, I will die a queen."

With a steady but firm voice she continued. "If he is ambitious, let Aurelian be told that I am ambitious, too—ambitious for a wider empire, for a greater fame, and for my people's love. Tell him I do not now speak of gratitude on the part of Rome, but maintain that the power which stood between Rome and Persia and saved the empire in the East, which twice pursued the Persian king even to the gates of his own capital, deserves some fairer acknowledgment from an ally whom its arms have thus

befriended than the message you now bring from
your Roman emperor."

The ambassadors were then summarily dismissed
and Zenobia prepared to defend her rights and her
kingdom. Nor did she permit Aurelian's legions to
approach the gates of Palmyra. She went a hundred
miles west to meet him, and two great battles were
fought, one near Antioch, the other near Emesa. In
both contests Zenobia herself led her troops of
archers and heavy cavalry, but they were no match
for the disciplined and experienced Roman soldiers.
Palmyra suffered defeats both times, and Zenobia
was forced to fall back within the gates of her capital
city.

Here she made a brave and last defense with
stones, arrows, and firebrands. So great was her courage that Aurelian was obliged to admit that she was
a most powerful and determined foe. He wrote of
her: "Those who speak with contempt of the war I
am waging against a woman are ignorant of both
the character and power of Zenobia." His offer of
advantageous terms for her surrender was rejected
by the proud queen as an insult. Zenobia hoped that
the Romans would tire of the siege and that her
eastern allies would come to her aid. Until then she
would hold out.

When food supplies began running short, however, the queen determined to escape and seek help

from Persia. Mounted on the fleetest of her dromedaries she succeeded in reaching the banks of the
Euphrates, sixty miles from Palmyra, but she was
pursued and taken captive and brought into the
presence of the Roman emperor.

Aurelian sternly demanded to know how she
dared continue to defy the power of Rome. Still
every inch a queen, she replied, "Because I dis-
dained to acknowledge as my masters such men as
your predecessors. You alone I recognize as my conqueror and my sovereign."

Aurelian spared the life of the heroic queen, since
he hoped she might be one of the show pieces of
his coming triumph in Rome. That she did not take
her own life as had Cleopatra appears to be more to
her credit than to her dishonor.

Once Palmyra had surrendered, Aurelian seized
its vast treasure and, leaving a garrison of six hundred archers, started back to Rome, carrying with
him as choice prizes Zenobia and her family. As he
was preparing to cross the Bosporus he received
word that the Palmyrans had revolted and massacred the garrison. He immediately retraced his steps
and ruthlessly sacked and destroyed the beautiful
city, his soldiers slaughtering all the inhabitants. The
gorgeous buildings were soon heaps of ruins, and
though he later repented of his fury and sought to
rebuild the city in part, he was too late.

When Aurelian finally returned to Rome in 273 a great parade was held in honor of his triumphs. Animals from all the empire came first, then the captured treasures and the offerings of the conquered nations. Finally came the long train of captives who were to become slaves of prominent Roman families.

Every eye turned upon Zenobia, queen of the East. Dressed in her royal robes and wearing her blazing jewels, she walked proudly in front of her golden chariot. Her arms were bound with chains of gold so heavy that a slave helped her carry them, but she bore herself with imperial grace.

The emperor was generous to his royal prisoner, giving her a handsome villa at Tivoli, twenty miles from Rome, where she lived out her years in honor as a Roman matron. Her daughters married into noble Roman families, and her youngest son became king of a part of Armenia.

Palmyra was never rebuilt, and again became an oasis and resting place for caravans as it had been in the days of King Solomon. Interest in the ancient city was revived in 1710 when the Swedish king sent an expedition to survey the ruins. In the early years of the present century German archaeologists began its restoration which has been continued by the French.

Some idea of the splendor of Palmyra in its years of greatness can be gained from these excavations.

One can imagine the colorful scene along the main street of colonnades as her subjects kneeled while their Queen Zenobia rode by on horseback, a majestic and powerful figure who dared to defy the greatest power in the world until overcome and taken prisoner.

4

Isabella of Spain

1451-1504

The greatest contribution of some monarchs to their kingdoms was laying the foundation for future greatness. During the fifteenth century Isabella and her consort, Ferdinand, prepared Spain to become a great unified nation. Often called "the Catholic," Isabella was devoted and steadfast in her support of the Roman Catholic Church.

For years after the great Mohammedan invasion in the eighth century, Spain was divided into many small states. In the fifteenth century these were united to form four large ones: Castile, Aragon, Navarre, and Granada. Of their once extensive possessions in the peninsula, only Granada remained to the Moors.

On April 22, 1451, in the palace of King John II
of Castile, a Spanish princess was born and christened Isabella. She was descended, on both her
mother's and her father's sides, from Alfred the
Great, William the Conqueror, the Plantagenet kings
of England, and St. Louis, king of France. Almost a
year later, on the tenth of March, 1452, in the little
town of Sos, a son was born to King John II of
Aragon, and named Ferdinand.

When Isabella was four years old, her father died,
and her half brother, Henry, became king of Castile
as Henry IV. Since she had another younger brother,
Alfonso, there seemed little probability that Isabella
would ever succeed to the throne. Her mother took
her from the court to the little town of Arevalo, and
she was given the education appropriate to a
daughter of the Spanish nobility, with particular
emphasis on religious subjects.

The princess's peaceful life, however, was sacri-
ficed to the ambition of her brother, and Isabella became a pawn on Henry's political chessboard. Without consulting his sister, he promised her in marriage
to a rich and dissolute middle-aged nobleman, Don
Pedro Girón, and elaborate preparations were made
for the wedding. The prospect of a forced marriage
to such a man was so depressing that the sixteen-
year-old girl seriously considered suicide.

Meanwhile, Don Pedro set out from his castle to

claim his youthful bride. But at the end of his first day's journey, he was seized with an attack of quinsy which proved fatal. He died three days later, and Isabella was happy again.

Isabella's brother Alfonso, who was next in succession to the throne, died soon after this. The nobles of Castile asked her to proclaim herself queen, dethroning Henry. Isabella refused, but the nobles were able to force the king to name her heiress to the throne, and to promise that she would not be compelled to marry against her will.

King Henry, however, almost immediately broke his promise and began negotiating a marriage between Isabella and Alfonso V, king of Portugal, threatening to imprison her unless she consented to the arrangement. But Isabella had two other suitors —the brother and heir apparent of King Louis XI of France, and Prince Ferdinand of Aragon, to whom she had once before in very early childhood been promised. Ferdinand was described by her chaplain, who was sent to investigate the young suitor, as "a very proper youth, comely in face and symmetrical in figure, with a spirit that is equal to anything he might desire to do."

Isabella's choice was made. To postpone giving an answer to her Portuguese suitor, she brought up the question of his kinship to her. It would require a special dispensation from Catholic Church authorities in Rome for them to be married. Meanwhile, knowing that King Henry would never approve of Ferdinand, she secretly sent couriers to accept his proposal. But King Henry learned of this and ordered her arrest. When the troops arrived to seize her, the citizens protected her while she fled to the palace at Madrigal.

Her messengers to Aragon returned with news both good and bad. Ferdinand had signed the marriage agreement on January 7, 1469, and sent her a dowry of jewels and gold coins, but he could not immediately come to Castile to marry her because of family and political conditions in Aragon. Again Henry sent a troop of royal cavalry to arrest Isabella. But two hours before they arrived at Madrigal, a dragoon regiment of the archbishop of Toledo came to her rescue. She was conducted to the town of Valladolid, fifty miles away near the northern border of Castile.

Isabella and the archbishop both realized that King Henry would eventually catch up with them and imprison her. She would be stopped if she attempted to cross the border to Aragon. Therefore Ferdinand must come to her; once they were married her brother could do nothing. So her fiancé was summoned.

Ferdinand made the trip disguised as a mule driver in a caravan of merchants (his friends and soldiers), joining his betrothed at Valladolid on the eleventh of October. They had never met before and were together for only two hours at this first encounter.

The next day the princess wrote to King Henry, telling him that she intended to marry Ferdinand and asking his blessing. No reply was received, but the wedding ceremony was performed by the archbishop of Toledo on October 19, 1469.

At the time of her marriage Isabella was eighteen and a half, a year older than Ferdinand, who was her second cousin. The archbishop had obtained the necessary papal dispensation for such a marriage within a family. Both were handsome and well educated and seemed to be perfect mates. As was customary in royal marriage contracts, Ferdinand agreed to several stipulations. He was to respect the laws of Castile, live there and never leave without Isabella's consent. If she succeeded King Henry, Ferdinand would be king in name only.

Ferdinand and Isabella were able to borrow enough on her dowry of jewels to defray the expenses of the wedding and establish their small court in a style which, while unusually simple for royalty, was adequate. A year after the wedding their first child, a daughter named for her mother, was born. Even then King Henry was not reconciled to the marriage, and refused to give Isabella the income from her royal lands. During the first years of marriage, Ferdinand was often absent, aiding his aged father in the rule of Aragon.

The couple's fortunes improved in 1474 when Henry died. Isabella was proclaimed queen of Castile. She was then twenty-three years old and at that time was in Segovia. On the thirteenth of December, riding on a thoroughbred horse, she led a procession to one of the public squares where a magnificent throne had been erected. To the accompaniment of the bells of the churches and convents throughout the city, a herald cried out, "Castile, Castile, for the king Don Fernando and his consort Doña Isabella, Queen Proprietor of these kingdoms! Hail the Queen!" and the people acclaimed their new monarch with cries of *"Viva la Reina!"*

When she had taken the oath of office, Isabella left immediately for the cathedral to pray that she would be a just and successful ruler.

Having been called to Aragon to put down a rebellion, Ferdinand was not present at these ceremonies. When he learned of his wife's coronation he rushed back to Segovia. He was highly displeased with the document prepared by the councilors of Castile, for it stipulated that Isabella was to be sole monarch. In spite of the fact that this had been one of the terms of their marriage agreement, he apparently thought that she would turn her throne over

to him as king or at least declare him heir to it. With
skill and diplomacy Isabella convinced him that, in
spite of legal titles, they would be ruling together,
for all official papers were to be signed jointly and
both their faces would appear on the Castilian seals
and coins.

The rulers began to reorganize the government of
Castile and to reestablish its prestige and power. Because they early showed their independence of him,
the archbishop of Toledo, who had long been their
champion and adviser and had assumed that they
would be his tools, turned against the couple. He
became an ally of the Portuguese king Alfonso V, who
had married the fifteen-year-old daughter of the late
King Henry and in 1475 claimed the titles of king
and queen of Castile.

To overcome this threat to her throne, Isabella
roused her subjects to her side, riding tirelessly
throughout the kingdom of Castile from fortress to
fortress to gain support in money and men. Forty-
two thousand soldiers were enlisted in the defense
of their queen. Ferdinand prepared them to move
against the Portuguese invaders, who had taken possession of the two leading Castilian strongholds of
Toro and Zamora.

A great battle was fought in February, 1476, on
a plain about five miles from Toro. The battle raged
all day and after the lances of both forces had been

broken, the soldiers fought hand to hand with swords. Ferdinand's horsemen attacked, re-formed, and attacked again with ever-increasing vigor. By sunset the retreat of the Portuguese became a rout; in attempting to cross the Douro River in a blinding rainstorm, scores were drowned. The victory at Toro was quickly followed by the recapture of Zamora. The kingdom was again secure.

During these troubled times, as in every crisis, Queen Isabella showed her absolute dependence upon prayer. Her religious faith was so strong that she asked God's guidance in every situation. When she received the news of this victory, she led a thanksgiving procession to the local church, walking barefoot and garbed as a penitent.

Ferdinand and Isabella ruled wisely, correcting many injustices, settling local disputes, and overcoming their rebel enemies and the numerous robber barons who caused continuous unrest. Within a few months the entire kingdom of Castile acknowledged the supremacy of the rulers. The birth of a son, Juan, in 1478 meant that Isabella had a male heir to the throne. When Alfonso invaded Castile again in 1479, Isabella was able to negotiate a treaty of friendship with Portugal.

Ferdinand's father, the king of Aragon, died in 1479, leaving the throne to his son. Aragon and Castile were thus united, and, though Ferdinand and

Isabella retained the separate administration of the two states, the great Spanish monarchy was founded. Now came a period when the two began to work toward the unification of all the states into one kingdom of Spain.

The last Spanish foothold of the Moors was in the state of Granada, and the two monarchs now set out to expel them. They were determined to end the Moorish domination which had existed for more than seven centuries and looked upon this as a Christian crusade, well aware that the war would be long and costly in both men and materiel.

Beginning in 1481, they systematically attacked the various Moorish strongholds by raids, skirmishes, and large-scale battles. But the Moors were prepared to defend the province of Granada to the death, and the Spaniards had to advance almost yard by yard.

Ferdinand and Isabella undertook this major enterprise jointly, each, however, having specific responsibilities. The king was to lead the army, the queen to raise funds and recruit and supply troops. One of her accomplishments was the importation of master gunners and engineers from Germany, France, and Italy. They obtained and developed the best artillery and munitions, and made the fullest possible use of the newly introduced gunpowder.

The first major military operation was against

the strongly fortified city of Málaga in May, 1487. Ferdinand first tried to obtain a surrender without bloodshed, making generous offers to the Moorish commander, who replied, "I am stationed here to defend the place to the last extremity. The Christian king cannot offer a bribe large enough to induce me to betray my trust."

With a force of seventy thousand soldiers, Ferdinand then laid siege to the city, surrounding it by sea and land. Knowing that her presence would inspire the Spaniards, Queen Isabella joined him and was received with joy. During the siege of three and a half months the troops were constantly reminded of the religious character of the operation, and Catholic rites were performed in camp with impressive ceremony. The religious discipline was so strong that swearing and gambling were severely punished.

Suffering from disease and famine, the citizens of Málaga finally admited their defeat and surrendered unconditionally. On the eighteenth of August, 1487, the Spanish army, with Ferdinand and Isabella at its head, entered the city and solemnized their victory in its cathedral. Ferdinand dealt harshly with the captive Moors: every citizen who could not pay a substantial ransom within eight months was to be sold into slavery. Eleven thousand Moors were thus enslaved.

For the next four years the Spanish pressed their

advance into the province of Granada, always meeting with unyielding resistance on the part of the
Moors, who inflicted tremendous losses on their attackers. Following the fall of Almería, the stronghold
of Baza was besieged for many months without success. Time and again Isabella had to pawn the crown
jewels to raise money for her husband's forces. At
length, as the Spanish troops became more and more
discouraged at their failure to capture the city, Ferdinand sent for his wife.

When Queen Isabella arrived at the camp, the
Spanish cavaliers gave her an enthusiastic reception.
The presence of this extraordinary woman, whose
character was a rare combination of feminine grace,
piety, self-reliance, and courage, lifted their spirits.
It also convinced the Moors that the Spanish army
would never withdraw until its foes surrendered.
Therefore, soon after the arrival of Isabella, the
Moorish garrison at Baza capitulated.

Granada, the capital of the province, was the last
stronghold still in the possession of the Moors. In
1491 Ferdinand encamped within four miles of the
city and began besieging it.

Queen Isabella always took an active part in the
military operations of the Spanish army. She often
appeared on the field wearing full armor and
mounted upon a noble Arabian horse. In the Spanish
camp near Granada she occupied a tent draped with

silken hangings. One night a gust of wind blew the fringes of a curtain into the lamp flame, setting fire to the entire tent. The fire spread to other tents, doing much damage before it was finally put out. To prevent the repetition of such an occurrence, Ferdinand ordered a city of substantial houses built upon the spot occupied by his army. Within three months a large city was completed. The soldier-builders wished to call it Isabella, in honor of their queen; but the devout Isabella named it Santa Fé, in recognition of her faith in God.

The Moors were finally forced to surrender Granada on January 2, 1492, but that date and year were to go down in history for another reason.

While the king and queen of Spain were at Santa Fé, a young man named Christopher Columbus arrived at their camp. The Atlantic Ocean was then largely unexplored. Columbus, who was employed in making maps and charts, was convinced that countries existed on the other side of the world, which he believed to be spherical, not flat. Through the prior of the monastery of La Rábida at Palos he appealed to Queen Isabella for money to finance an expedition. The prior wrote the monarch a letter which impressed her so much that she asked Columbus to come to Santa Fé. By a happy coincidence he arrived on the very day of the capitulation of Granada.

Columbus asked for only a few ships and a few

sailors. He wanted to find a new and shorter route to India, trade with which was then the greatest source of European wealth. The royal finances of Spain were depleted by war, and at first the queen refused his request. Columbus departed, saying he would make the same offer to the king of France. But Isabella was so struck by the dream of Columbus that she decided to pledge her private jewels to raise the necessary funds.

On the third of August, 1492, Christopher Columbus' small squadron of three ships unfurled its sails for the momentous voyage. On October 12 he landed at one of the islands of the Bahamas, which he renamed San Salvador. Two months later he arrived in Haiti, to which he gave the name of Hispaniola. During the following decade Columbus led three other expeditions to the Caribbean, claiming for Spain what are now the islands of Puerto Rico, Jamaica, and Trinidad. He also landed at Honduras. These voyages sponsored by Queen Isabella were the beginnings of the Spanish colonial empire in the new world.

After an active and courageous life devoted to the interest of her kingdom, Queen Isabella died in November, 1504. Her two oldest children had died before her, Isabella in 1498 and Juan in 1497. Juana, the oldest of the three surviving daughters, became queen of Castile. Since she was insane, her husband, the archduke of Austria, ruled in her name as Philip I. When he died in 1506, Ferdinand, who had governed Castile for Philip and Juana while they were in Flanders, became regent for their six-year-old son Charles. He also continued to rule his own kingdom of Aragon, uniting it with Navarre, until his death in 1516. Juana lived on, in solitary confinement, until 1555. The two other surviving daughters of Ferdinand and Isabella were both married to kings— Maria to Emanuel I of Portugal and Catherine to Henry VIII of England.

Queen Isabella had changed the course of Spain's history, uniting two of the states and recapturing the third, Granada, from the Moors. Unlike many queens, Isabella was fortunate in having a husband who was both a helpmate and a partner in all her endeavors. Their motto, "the one as much as the other," indicated this closeness. Rarely have a king and queen worked together so harmoniously. Unfortunately, Isabella's accomplishments are shadowed by the dreadful Inquisition, established in 1480, which in Spain was both political and religious. However, this phase of her life must be judged in the context of her devotion to the church and what she deemed to be its best interests. Her contributions to Spain as a nation cannot be questioned. She unified the country under a strong central government and, by supporting the first explorations, set the stage for the expansion of the empire which was to make Spain the greatest power in Europe during the sixteenth century.

5

Catherine de' Medici

1519-1589

Catherine de' Medici has gone down in history as a queen devoid of every womanly instinct, every womanly virtue, every womanly characteristic. Of her it has been said that no man or woman has ever lived with less conscience and fewer scruples.

But before judging her it is important to remember her environment and education. The ideal ruler of the sixteenth century was a tyrant, as pictured in Niccolò Machiavelli's *The Prince*. Completely lacking morality, the ideal ruler would use boldness, force, fraud, or cruelty to gain his desired ends. Catherine's villainies were indeed terrible, but quite possibly she has been accused of other crimes of which she was innocent.

Catherine was the daughter of Lorenzo de' Medici, nephew of Pope Leo X and a member of the powerful ruling family of Florence, Italy. Her mother died a fortnight after her birth and her father six days later. Her childhood was spent in convents. Her uncle, Pope Clement VII, and Francis I, the king of France, arranged a marriage between Catherine and the king's second son, Henry of Orleans. The marriage was celebrated in 1533 when Catherine was only fourteen and her husband a little over fifteen years old.

She was a thick-set, plain, unprepossessing girl, and being so young, a foreigner, and a native of a state having no great weight in the world of politics, was pushed into the background by more attractive and important members of the French court. She was always called "the Italian woman" and viewed with suspicion.

As in all such arranged marriages, young Catherine neither expected nor received much attention from her boy-husband. Her father-in-law, however, took a great liking to her. But the prejudice against her persisted and even grew. When Henry's older brother, Francis, died in 1536, Catherine was accused of having poisoned him so that her husband would be dauphin, the next in line for the throne.

In 1540, when he was twenty-two, Henry fell desperately in love with the famed Diane de Poitiers, a widow who was twenty years older than he. At this early period of Henry's attachment for her, Diane derived from it no influence at court, for King Francis I disliked his second son. While Diane professed a motherly affection for the young man, Catherine looked on seemingly unmoved. For twenty years she was forced to take second place to her husband's paramour.

Catherine's first child, Francis, was not born until the tenth year of her marriage, and nine others, three of whom died in babyhood, were born in the next eleven years. Of her four sons, three were to reign in succession in France as Francis II, Charles IX, and Henry III.

King Francis I died in 1547 and Catherine's husband was crowned as Henry II. During his twelve-year reign Catherine de' Medici showed no outward signs of displeasure with her royal husband. He continued under the influence of Diane de Poitiers, who was known to hold the power of a monarch. Catherine silently waited her turn, carefully observing the various moves of the political game then being played in Europe. Though she affected not only tolerance but friendship for Diane, the crafty Catherine was merely biding her time.

The reign of Francis I had left France in a weak position. Henry decided to declare war on Germany and Spain in the hope of recouping some of France's

power. Before leaving Paris for the German campaign he made his wife regent of France, a move
which surprised Catherine because it was the first
time that he had paid any attention to her in matters
of state. Henry took good care, however, to tie her
hands so that she was actually regent in name only,
while Diane held most of the real power.

Henry II departed with his army and with ease
took possession of the German-held cities of Metz,
Toul, and Verdun. Meanwhile the Spaniards had
invaded France and ignominiously defeated the
main French army in a desperately fought battle at
Saint-Quentin in 1557.

This was the time when Catherine first had an
opportunity to display her political tact and personal
courage. When the news of the capture of Saint-
Quentin reached Paris, a great panic seized the citizens. Many of them, realizing that the enemy was
approaching, fled in terror. Catherine refused to be
frightened. She went to Parliament, urged them not
to lose heart but to go ahead vigorously with the
war, and to vote immediate subsidies for the kingdom. So stirring was her appeal that she received an
immense ovation, Parliament immediately granting
100,000 crowns to raise the necessary troops.

Because of the ascendancy of Diane de Poitiers,
this was the first time that the queen had used her
royal power, and it did much to overcome the wide-

spread prejudice against her as a foreigner. From that day Catherine's position was changed. Henry was greatly impressed, and began to show her respect and attention, continuing to do so for the remaining two years of his life. During the next year their eldest son Francis was married to Mary, Queen of Scots. Both of them were fifteen years old.

The king's relationship with Diane, however, continued as strong as ever, and he wore her colors in tournaments, which were currently very popular. In these, armed knights galloped at each other and strove to break the opponent's lance. In 1559, a tournament was held celebrating his daughter Elizabeth's marriage to Philip II of Spain. The king invited the count of Montgomery, a lieutenant in the Scottish guards, to break a lance with him. The visor of Henry's helmet was not properly adjusted, and Montgomery's lance pierced the monarch's eye. Blood poisoning set in and the king died in eleven days. So great and genuine was his wife's grief for him, faithless and inconsiderate as he had been, that for the rest of her life Catherine de' Medici wore black only.

Her first act as regent was to order Diane de Poitiers from the court. She eagerly seized the reins of power, and was able to develop her abilities during the reigns of her sons. Francis II, who succeeded his father at the age of sixteen, ruled for only a year and a half. At his death his ten-year-old brother became king as Charles IX, reigning for fourteen years.

By the middle of the sixteenth century all Europe was agitated by the controversy between Catholics and Protestants. The writings of Luther, Calvin, and other reformers had aroused the Christian world. Now the religious conflict spread from Germany, where it had literally torn the country apart, to France. At first Catherine attempted to conciliate the differences between the two factions, but the controversy raged on, eventually erupting into warfare.

The first of the civil wars of religion began in 1562. France became the arena where the Catholics and Protestants of Europe hurled themselves against each other. As regent for the boy-king Charles IX, Catherine headed the Catholics. Jeanne d'Albret, queen of Navarre, and a Huguenot—Protestants were called Huguenots in France—was recognized as the head of the Protestant leaders. There were frequent skirmishes and battles, followed by months of apparent peace, negotiations for which were generally undertaken by Catherine. Many thousands of Protestants perished in massacres, and individuals were more and more persecuted.

Becoming stronger, the Catholics prepared for a decisive engagement which would settle the religious question once and for all. The Protestants were defeated in 1568 in a bloody battle, but remained undaunted, rallying their forces anew around the brave queen of Navarre. The opposing forces met for a second time, and again the Protestants were overcome. Jeanne, with the help of Germany, organized a third army, and this time the tide turned in her favor. Catherine was forced to sue for peace, a proposition which the Protestants gladly accepted. The terms of the treaty gave Protestants the freedom to worship and to hold public office on the same terms as the Catholics. France momentarily quieted down.

Now Catherine de' Medici lavished attentions on Jeanne's son, young Henry of Navarre, hoping to convert him to Catholicism. King Charles, then twenty, was betrothed to Elizabeth, daughter of the Emperor Maximilian II of Austria, and Catherine used the occasion of the wedding festivities to offer Henry the hand of her daughter Margaret. This alliance, it was hoped, would please both Protestants and Catholics. Jeanne d'Albret felt that such a marriage would protect the Huguenots from further persecution and save France from continued bloodshed.

Jeanne arrived in Paris in June, 1572, to complete the wedding arrangements, but she became ill and died within nine days. The report spread that Catherine had poisoned the queen of Navarre. This accusation was subsequently disproved, but not before it had done its damage. Jeanne's death delayed the marriage, but in August the ceremony was performed. Paris was filled with Protestant notables who had come from all parts of Europe for the occasion, hoping against hope that this marriage might heal the wounds of the wars of religion and bring the adherents of both religions firmly together.

But the animosities had at best only been concealed, and the inflammable situation erupted into violence four days after the wedding. Admiral Coligny, a leading French Protestant and a close friend of Henry of Navarre, was the first victim. As he was passing through the streets of Paris, he was shot from a window. One bullet entered his left arm, and another severed a finger of his right hand. Rumors of plans for retaliation were everywhere. One rumor was that the Huguenots planned an uprising to seize the throne.

To Catherine the only possible answer to this rebellion against the throne of France was the destruction of the Protestants. She felt that the extermination of the Huguenots would prevent another bloody and disruptive religious civil war. Her plan was cold-blooded, but Charles, frightened by rumors that he was to be murdered, eagerly joined his mother.

At two o'clock on the morning of August 24, 1572, while Catherine and Charles watched from one of the apartments in the Louvre, the fatal signal rang out and armed Catholics rushed into the streets of Paris, shouting, *"Vive Dieu et le roi!"*

The terrible butchery which followed is known in history as the Massacre of Saint Bartholomew because it occurred upon the anniversary of a festival in the saint's honor.

The first victim was the wounded Coligny. Helpless and abandoned by his frightened servants, he was murdered and thrown from the window of his lodging. Everywhere the streets resounded with cries of "Kill! Kill!" The massacre continued for an entire week, and it is estimated that two thousand Protestants were murdered in Paris alone, and many other thousands throughout the kingdom.

From every part of Europe arose a cry of horror. Queen Elizabeth of England shrouded her court in mourning and refused to give audience to the French ambassador. But no emotions of regret or sorrow moved the heart of Catherine de' Medici; she always felt that the massacre was necessary and justified.

Two years later, in 1574, Charles died, crying remorsefully, "What evil counsels I have followed! Oh, my God, forgive me them!" When her third and favorite son, Henry, ascended the French throne as Henry III, Catherine found that her power was weakening. He was impatient of her control, refusing to accept her guidance, and she soon realized that he would not be a pliant tool in her hands. Together they ruled for fifteen years. Catholics and Protestants again began warring against one another. The Catholics formed a league under the brave but unprincipled duke of Guise, who had led the massacre.

There were now three Henrys: Henry III, king of France; Henry, king of Navarre; and Henry, duke of Guise. The war which followed is called the War of the Three Henrys, a struggle for personal power in which religious prejudices played a major role. During it, Henry of Guise was assassinated on the king's order and in his presence. Henry III boasted of this deed to his mother, saying, "I have made myself this morning king of France by putting to death the king of Paris," which was the title given to the duke of Guise.

"Take care," Catherine replied, "that you do not soon find yourself the king of nothing." She realized the awfulness of this crime against her most zealous worker, and said, "May God annihilate me, may He damn me, if I ever dreamed this crime or counseled it!"

Twelve days later the queen died friendless and unmourned in the castle of Blois. "She has done much good and evil in her day," a Paris priest told his congregation, adding, "more evil, I think, than good." She left France demoralized and in the throes of civil war, her name despised alike by Catholics and Protestants.

Seven months after the death of his mother, Henry III, the last of her sons, was assassinated by a monk, and Henry of Navarre was proclaimed king of France.

All of Catherine de' Medici's scheming had come to naught. She and her sons died with the curses of the nation upon their heads, while the son of the Protestant Jeanne d'Albret sat upon the throne of France.

Modern students of psychology have sought to explain Catherine's actions as the result of her long personal unhappiness and neglect, first as an orphan, then as a wife humiliated by the continuous presence and power of her husband's mistress. She also always felt keenly the uneasiness and suspicion which her foreign birth aroused in the French. The power which came to her enabled her to take revenge for these injustices.

On the other hand, Catherine de' Medici possessed tremendous personal ambition and thoroughly enjoyed wielding the power which was hers as queen mother and regent. The religious conflicts, which she honestly attempted to mediate, finally forced her to abandon the role of peacemaker and ally herself with the Catholics rather than sacrifice the throne to her Protestant enemies.

In the end she was a weary, disappointed woman, beaten in all her plots.

6

Elizabeth I

1533-1603

One of the high points in English history was reached in the reign of Queen Elizabeth. The forty-five years from 1558 to 1603 have become known as the "Elizabethan age," a period when a surge of nationalism united the country in a pride of achievement. Elizabeth had found England weak and divided, and she left it strong and united. Religious toleration replaced persecution. Without continuous wars, England became the wealthiest and most influential country of Europe.

⇀ Rarely has a ruler been as well loved as "Good Queen Bess," and rarely has a monarch deserved such devotion. She was so attached to her beloved

England that she never ventured beyond its boundaries, not even to Scotland or Wales. -

In fact, she was never more than a hundred and fifty miles from Greenwich Palace, where she was born on September 7, 1533. She was the daughter of Henry VIII and his second wife, Anne Boleyn. Henry was bitterly disappointed at not having had a son and male heir, but he had Elizabeth christened by the church and recognized as a true "Princess of England."

Anne failed to produce a male heir, and Henry contrived a trial for adultery which resulted in her being beheaded when Elizabeth was not yet three years old. The day after the execution Henry married Jane Seymour, Anne's lady-in-waiting, who later gave birth to a son, Edward. The first public ceremony in which Elizabeth participated was his christening. She was just four, and marched in the procession, holding the hand of her half sister, Princess Mary, daughter of Catherine of Aragon, Henry's first wife, whom he had divorced. Jane died when Edward was but a week old. For some time Elizabeth lived in the same palace with the baby Edward, and she showed great affection for him.

After two more marriages, neither of which produced an heir, Henry in 1543 took as his sixth wife Catherine Parr. The new queen was beautiful, charming, and intelligent, and for the first time ten-year-old Elizabeth received the maternal love and security she had thus far lacked.

When Henry VIII died in 1547, his son Edward was crowned king as Edward VI. But this young monarch died of consumption six years later, when he was sixteen. The mighty realm of England was left, according to the terms of Henry's will, to Mary.

After her accession to the throne in August, 1553, the new queen's first Parliament revoked the divorce of her parents, Henry VIII and the Catholic Catherine of Aragon. In effect this made Elizabeth officially illegitimate. Mary also restored the supremacy of the Roman Catholic Church, and, to make England safe for Catholicism, married Philip of Spain.

Princess Elizabeth became the unwitting tool of the Protestants, who attempted a rebellion with the object of putting her on the throne in place of her half sister. Though she knew nothing of the plot, she was imprisoned for two months in the Tower of London and later taken to the royal residence of Woodstock, where she was given more freedom. Her correspondence, however, was carefully watched, and it was with great difficulty that she succeeded at length in appealing for the favor of the queen. While she was at Woodstock she scratched upon her window with a diamond the lines:

Much suspected, by me
Nothing proved can be,
Quoth Elizabeth, prisoner.

Through these years of unhappiness, Philip had been planning a future for Elizabeth, who was next in succession to the throne. When Queen Mary continued to be childless, he attempted to marry the princess to his Catholic ally, the duke of Savoy, but she refused the proposal. Later, when Elizabeth became queen, she rejected Philip's own proposal of marriage, and they were eventually to become deadly enemies.

Mary's reign was marked by intense persecution of the Protestants. So many heretics were burned at the stake or beheaded in her attempt to restore Catholicism as the state religion of England that she was given the title Bloody Mary. When Mary died without an heir in 1558, Elizabeth became the new queen. Fortunately, she had already learned, through the intrigues surrounding her while she was a princess, the lessons of caution and patience. Her youth had been lived in an atmosphere of jealousy, suspicion, and danger, and she determined from the start to rule more wisely than had her half sister.

On her first visit to London after her accession, Elizabeth, according to custom, went to visit the Tower of London. As she looked at the room where she once had been held prisoner, she said, "Some have fallen from being princes in this land to be prisoners in this place. I am raised from being prisoner in this place to be a prince of this land; so I must yield myself thankful to God and merciful to man, in remembrance of the same."

Elizabeth's coronation took place two months after her accession, on Sunday, January 15, 1559, when she was twenty-five. Wearing a crimson velvet robe, a cap of gold and pearls, and a small ermine cape, she walked into Westminster Abbey on a carpet of royal purple. With her very fair skin, her naturally curly reddish hair, and big golden-brown eyes, she looked lovely as well as regal. She was crowned with the traditional crown of St. Edward, the state crown, and with the little crown that had been made for the coronation of her ten-year-old brother Edward.

The new queen realized that her position as a Protestant queen must be established immediately. The Catholics felt that she had no right to the crown. In fact, the Pope himself had forbidden her to become queen. As a result, her first Parliament, ten days after her coronation, enacted the "Act of Supremacy." The Church of England was firmly reestablished as the official state church. The Latin mass was no longer permitted, and the English prayerbook was adopted officially. This legislation was intended to settle the troublesome religious question by suppressing Catholicism.

Proposals for the new queen's hand poured in from every court of Europe, but Elizabeth rejected them all, then and always. Throughout her reign, emissaries from the countries of Europe arrived to negotiate a marriage with the English queen. She took a genuine delight in deceiving her suitors into believing that she intended to marry them. She would hold off her answer, teasing them into paying her court, before she finally made her inevitable negative decision.

From time to time Parliament would officially request that she marry, but she always evaded the issue. Once, taking off her coronation ring and holding it up, she told them, "When I received this ring I solemnly bound myself in marriage to the realm." She was not above showing her authority when annoyed by their persistence in the subject. When the House of Lords brought up the question one time, she retorted, "Did I so choose I might make the impertinence of the whole lot of you an excuse to withdraw any idea of marriage. But for the realm's sake I am resolved that I will take a husband, and he will not be to the taste of some of you."

For eleven years Archduke Charles of Austria was an expectant suitor, but the final excuse was the difference of religion. Catherine de' Medici put forth her son, the nineteen-year-old duke of Anjou, later

Henry III of France, as a candidate when Elizabeth was thirty-seven, to no avail. Then Catherine's youngest son, Francis, the duke of Alençon, Elizabeth's junior by twenty-one years, wooed her for ten years without success. This was her last courtship, and it reached the stage of the drawing up of a marriage contract. Elizabeth gave him her pledge with a ring, and the date of the wedding was set. But at the last moment the queen used her royal prerogative of changing her mind. Throughout the years there were also many suitors among the English nobility.

The man whom she probably really wished to marry was Robert Dudley, but he was a commoner, already married. When his wife died in an accident, many believed him guilty of murdering her. Though she finally decided against marriage, Elizabeth made him earl of Leicester. He remained for many years one of her most faithful and devoted advisers, a member of the Privy Council. Leicester served his queen well through periods of favor and disfavor, finally becoming lieutenant general of the armed forces.

Elizabeth was completely at home in the company of men, and it was said that her mind functioned like a man's, logically and unemotionally. The queen's wit and speech, robust and often coarse, made the men around her feel comfortable in her presence.

She disliked being crossed and had a weakness for flattery. Those who were close to her were forced to develop the art.

Elizabeth's government was well managed. She possessed the ability to call forth the best in her ministers and advisers. Most of her statesmen were able. Lord Burghley was her secretary of state for forty years, and Sir Nicholas Bacon and his more famous son, Francis, were among her wise and remarkable ministers.

Elizabeth was always conscious of her Tudor heritage, and proved to be proud and fearless. Early in her reign she said to an ambassador, "Although I may not be a lion, I am a lion cub, and I have a lion's heart." She became adept in exercising caution, a lesson learned in her unhappy childhood. She weighed her words, but when the time came to speak there was no question of her opinions or the authority behind them.

She could also be temperamental, for she would speak pleasantly, all smiles and good will, and then suddenly give vent to uncontrolled anger and turn upon the unsuspecting object of her wrath. "When she smiled," wrote her godson, Sir John Harrington, of her, "it had a pure sunshine that every one did choose to bask in if they could. But anon came a sudden gathering of clouds, and the thunder fell in a wondrous manner on all."

Her disfavor was much to be feared. Yet, when agreeable, she could employ great charm. "The queen did fish for men's souls," one of her advisers wrote, "and had so sweet a bait that no one could escape from her net."

Elizabeth's hold on Parliament was secure. She spoke to the members of the Houses of Commons and Lords as a king, not as a woman. Never were they in doubt as to who held the real power of England. When their wishes were contrary to hers, she railed against them and accused them of "unparalleled audacity" and disloyalty. Once, for example, she expressed her displeasure in their acts by dissolving Parliament. "Let this discipline," she told them, "stand you in stead of sorer strokes, never to tempt too far a ruler's patience. . . . Your return to our grace will call to your minds that we are always alert to your best interests."

But above all, Elizabeth the Queen was complete in her devotion to her subjects and her nation. Immediately after her coronation she charged her newly appointed judges with these words: "You have my people. Do you that which I ought to do. They cannot avenge themselves, nor help themselves. See unto them, for they are my charge. I care not for myself; my life is not dear to me. My care is for my people. . . ." And, after the defeat of the Spanish Armada, she said to a London street crowd:

"Ye may have a greater prince, but ye shall never have a more loving prince."

Looking for the first time beyond its own borders, England during the reign of Elizabeth began advances in exploration and the expansion of trade. The discoveries of Columbus in the 1490's, Magellan and Balboa in the early 1500's, and Cortez, Pizarro, and Coronado a little later, had given Spain an imposing number of colonies—Cuba, Mexico, and the north coast of South America, called the Spanish Main. At the beginning of Elizabeth's reign, Spain was the leading world power.

To share the riches of the new world England needed either to gain a foothold in the new lands or to take over some of the trade routes established by the Spanish. Sir Francis Drake epitomized this new spirit of British expansion, in the main aimed against the implacable Spanish enemy.

Drake's first voyage to the Caribbean in 1570 resulted in plunder from the Spanish colonies. But the unknown vastness of the Pacific presented a challenge to him. In 1577 Drake embarked with five ships on a three-year voyage up the coast of California; but the expedition eventually took him around the world and yielded great riches from captured Spanish ships. He discovered Cape Horn on this trip. Later he made other voyages to Mexico and the Caribbean.

After a long and persistent study of ocean currents and winds, Humphrey Gilbert, a geographer, advanced a theory that there was a northwest passage to India, which would be much shorter than that used by the Spanish and Portuguese. Between 1576 and 1578 Queen Elizabeth licensed three voyages by Martin Frobisher to search for such a passage. Although he failed in his primary purpose, he did discover a bay in Canada, afterward to be called Frobisher Bay.

Gilbert believed that a colony might be established on the American coast, and in 1578 he obtained a six-year monopoly of discovery and settlement in America. In 1583 he arrived at Newfoundland and took possession in the name of Elizabeth. The next year (1584) Sir Walter Raleigh, Gilbert's half brother, received a similar patent, and sent out an expedition which landed on Roanoke Island. The region was named Virginia in honor of Elizabeth "The Virgin Queen."

Meanwhile Sir John Hawkins, a slave merchant, and other sea captains were roaming the Atlantic and Pacific, everywhere striking at Spanish merchant vessels and seeking to win control of the flourishing trade. Seizures of Spanish galleons yielded great riches, and the voyages of plunder were undertaken with the blessing and encouragement of the queen, who invested money in them.

While English explorers and traders were sailing the seas, Elizabeth's kingdom was prospering at home. A wealthy leisure class arose which provided patrons for writers. Henry VIII had developed an extensive system of private schools, so the members of this class were well educated. As a result, in Elizabethan times literature flowered as never before in England. It was the age of geniuses such as Edmund Spenser, Christopher Marlowe, and, towering above all, William Shakespeare. Elizabeth's reign is often called the "golden age of English literature."

The contemporary spirit of exploration and adventure was an impetus to literature, and mirrored the pride of nationality. Much of the literary work was patriotic, heroic, romantic, and adventurous. One result of this national pride and interest in the world was an extensive publication of historical and geographical works, or "chronicles," of which Richard Hakluyt's work on current explorations was the most popular. The stories of the past monarchs as recounted in Holinshed's *Chronicles* (1578) glorified the heritage of the Elizabethans.

Poetical works of all types were plentiful—lyrics, sonnets, satirical verse, and epics. The most famous single poem was Edmund Spenser's *The Faerie Queene*, one of the greatest long poems in the English language. The work was dedicated to Queen Elizabeth, "the most high, mighty, and magnificent

Empress, renowned for Piety, Virtue and all Gracious Government." It was to have been an allegory, set in King Arthur's time, on the twelve cardinal virtues of the perfect knight. But only six cantos were completed, three in 1590 and three in 1596. Elizabeth was represented in the character of Gloriana.

The most popular form of Elizabethan literature, however, was drama. The contemporary plays were designed for the common people, who were unable to read but who could stand in the outdoor theater pits and enjoy performances without stage settings. No less than eleven theaters were located in or near London at the time, and strolling players roamed throughout the kingdom.

The plays were of all types—comedy, tragedy, and historical drama. Before the days of Shakespeare, Christopher Marlowe was considered the first dramatist, and many believe that he might have rivaled the great Shakespeare himself had he not died at the age of twenty-nine.

William Shakespeare was not only the outstanding literary figure of his time, but also the greatest writer in all English literature and acknowledged as the greatest writer of drama in any language. His contemporary popularity was largely due to the vividness and universality of his characters and the superb representation of human strengths and weaknesses exhibited in them. Twenty-two of his plays were written and thirteen produced during Elizabeth's reign, beginning in 1590, but he continued to write until 1611.

Shakespeare's plays were of all types, each bearing the stamp of his genius. He told the story of the English monarchy in his historical "chronicle" plays. The comedies always included some lowborn characters who produced rollicking laughter, and the tragedies were impressive in both character and plot. Shakespeare was also an actor, and Elizabeth many times saw him perform in his own compositions.

Other great dramatists such as Ben Jonson, Beaumont and Fletcher, Heywood, and Webster, began their work during Elizabeth's reign and continued their productivity afterward.

Elizabethan England was also famous for its music. Four favorite instruments were used—the lute, the viol (predecessor of the violin), the virginal (predecessor of the piano), and the recorder (a type of flute). Every well-bred person was expected to be able to perform on at least one of them. Madrigals and part songs were popular, and group singing by families and friends was a part of leisure. The works of the leading composers—Thomas Tallis, William Byrd, and Orlando Gibbons—were for both instrument and voice.

Though sternly repressed, the Catholics were still numerous in Elizabethan England. If loyal to Rome, they could not openly support Elizabeth, who had been excommunicated in 1570 by a papal bull in which she was called a pretender. This document also freed the English Catholics "from their oath and all manner of duty, fidelity, and obedience" to her.

Mary, Queen of Scots (Mary Stuart), the most prominent Catholic, was a thorn in Elizabeth's side for most of her reign. Mary wanted to be named heir to the throne of England. But Elizabeth was unwilling to arouse the displeasure of her Protestant subjects and refused. When Mary Stuart abdicated the Scottish throne in favor of her son and escaped to England, hoping to find her way to France, Elizabeth kept her a prisoner for nineteen years. Mary was finally convicted of high treason and sentenced to death.

Some have condemned Elizabeth for her treatment of Mary. But behind her actions was a desire for peace: Mary might readily have stirred up a war with France, a Catholic country whose queen she had once been. And Spain, too, was a Catholic enemy. The beheading of Mary in February, 1587, was the signal for Spanish action against England, for she willed her claim to the English throne to King Philip II of Spain.

A continuing ambition of Philip, widower of Mary Tudor, was to reestablish Roman Catholicism in his former wife's kingdom and in the Netherlands. In 1585, in order to forestall open conflict with Spain, Elizabeth gave military and financial aid to the Netherlands (present-day Holland and Belgium) to aid in driving out the Spanish invaders. But the war became inevitable on Mary Stuart's death.

If successful in conquering England, Philip could ask the Pope to declare him the lawful heir to its throne. At the same time, the continued forays against the Spanish merchant fleet would be avenged, and Elizabeth would be punished for her help to the rebellious Dutch. He counted on the assistance of English and Scottish Catholics on the soil of England. The Spanish plan was to send the Invincible Armada to invade England.

When the danger of imminent invasion was made known, Elizabeth's subjects forgot their differences in religion and rallied to act against the common danger. The famed sea captains of the period put at the queen's disposal a fleet of eighty vessels, only four of which equaled in tonnage the smallest of the enemy galleons. The confidence of the English lay in the greater speed of their smaller ships, the size and number of their guns, and the experienced seamanship of the officers and men. This was to be the time for a final stand against a confident and overwhelmingly superior enemy, the greatest of the contemporary European powers. A volunteer army was quickly trained and assembled on the Channel shore to meet any invaders as they attempted to land.

During the last week of July, 1588, the Armada of 130 vessels, with 22,000 soldiers aboard, sailed slowly up the English Channel in crescent formation. The fleet planned to seize and hold the port of Plymouth while the Spanish soldiers in the Netherlands were ferried over to participate in an armed invasion. To drive the enemy from their shores, the English, with their faster ships, began pursuit. For eight days, in a running sea fight, the valiant Englishmen inflicted so much damage that the battered ships of the Armada sought refuge across the Channel in the harbor of Calais, France.

But several English fire ships were sent in among them and forced the fleet from its shelter into battle with the waiting enemy. The remains of the Spanish Armada could only try to get home by way of the passage to the north of Scotland and Ireland. In what the English ever afterward called "the Protestant wind," the Armada met violent gales and lost over fifty ships. Less than half the original fleet, shattered and crippled, managed to reach Spain.

Immediately after the great triumph, while there was still danger of a land invasion by the Spanish army from the Netherlands, Queen Elizabeth visited her assembled troops at Tilbury. After reviewing them, she addressed the five thousand soldiers who were to defend her shores. "I have always placed my strength and safeguard in the loyal hearts and good will of my subjects," she said. "I am resolved to live or die amongst you all, to lay down for God, or for my kingdom, and for my people, my honor and my blood, even in the dust. I know I have but the body of a weak and feeble woman, but I have the heart and stomach of a king, and of a king of England, too. . . ." With such words, it is not to be wondered at that her subjects were generally unswerving in their loyalty and devotion to her.

To the Spanish the defeat of their Armada was an immense national disaster, since it meant also the end of their sea power. For the English the victory was a lasting source of national pride. England was safe and with it the cause of Protestantism. This was the climax of Elizabeth's reign, and her subjects glorified her as the embodiment of the English spirit. Seldom had England been so united in the spirit of nationalism.

Throughout her reign Elizabeth was proud of the strong affection of her subjects. But she dreaded the approach of middle and old age. As she lost her good looks, she tried in every way to hide the marks of age. She wore elaborate wigs, huge ruffs, and lavishly trimmed and jeweled costumes to draw attention from the wrinkles of her face. Finally, she banned all mirrors from her palaces.

More and more Elizabeth surrounded herself with young men. The second of her celebrated favorites—the first had been Robert Dudley, the earl of Leicester—was Robert Devereux, earl of Essex. He was only twenty, the queen fifty-three, when their friendship began. Elizabeth was infatuated with him. But though Essex curried her favor, treating her with gallantry and charm, and was usually deferential to her, he resented her possessiveness and dictation. Their relationship, lasting fifteen years, was tempestuous, for the queen's emotions were mercurial.

In 1596 she sent Essex as commander of land forces to retake Cádiz, in which he was successful. Two years later he was sent to Ireland to put down a rebellion. Instead of battling the forces of the earl of Tyrone, which far outnumbered his own, Essex agreed to a truce on terms highly favorable to the Irish. Elizabeth was so highly displeased with him that she imprisoned him in the Tower for ten months, and after his release he was banned from the court.

Smarting at his loss of prestige and favor, Essex was rash enough to plot against the throne. After a trial for sedition, he and his fellow conspirators were condemned to death and beheaded in 1601.

As Elizabeth approached her seventieth year, her health began failing. She became weaker and weaker, but refused to take to her bed lest she be considered dying. At length she was so weak that she could no longer speak, but by signs she asked the archbishop of Canterbury to pray by her side. She died on March 24, 1603.

Elizabeth's forty-five years on the throne had been the longest reign in English history since that of Edward III in the fourteenth century. Her many good qualities as a ruler more than offset her weaknesses as a woman. Her devotion to England was her life, and under her it rose from a small, second-class power to become the greatest and most prosperous nation in Europe.

Charles Dickens characterized her reign in these words: "Elizabeth's reign had been a glorious one, and is made forever memorable by the distinguished men who flourished in it—the great voyagers, statesmen, scholars, and writers. It was a great reign for discovery, for commerce, and for English enterprise and spirit in general. It was a great reign for the Protestant religion and for the Reformation which made England free."

In Europe in the second half of the sixteenth century, four women governed their countries. Three of them—Mary of England, Mary, Queen of Scots, and Catherine de' Medici of France—left their countries worse than they found them. The fourth ruler, Elizabeth I, was the exception. As her legacy she passed on to her successor James I a secure and united nation.

7

Mary, Queen of Scots

1542-1587

Few queens have been as controversial as
Mary Stuart, ill-fated sovereign of Scotland. Her
partisans in her own day and later have been fervent
in their support and defense, her enemies equally
zealous in their unqualified condemnation. She was
the target of jealousy, treachery, and persecution, yet
she was a formidable plotter, an ambitious and beautiful woman who seemed doomed to unhappiness
and misfortune.

This queen was born on December 7, 1542, in the
castle of Linlithgow, the only child of James V of
Scotland and Mary of Guise, daughter of a noble
French Catholic house of Lorraine. As a great-grand-
daughter of Henry VII of England, she was next in

line for the English throne after the children of
Henry VIII.

When she was six days old her father died without
ever having seen her. Mary's coronation took place
when she was nine months old. From the very beginning she became a pawn of the Scottish nobles in
their political intrigues. King Henry VIII of England
demanded a contract for a marriage between the
infant queen and his five-year-old son, Prince Edward (later Edward VI), to take place when she was
ten years old. All the Scottish border fortresses were
to be surrendered immediately to show the good
faith of the Scots. The main purpose of the negotiations was thus exposed as the annexation of Scotland
to England, which to the Scots was out of the question. The contract was refused and British troops invaded Scotland in 1544. For the next four years, in
order to keep her from being kidnaped by the English, Mary was hidden in convents and monasteries.

Mary was betrothed to Francis, the dauphin and
heir to the French throne, and she went to the court
of Henry II and Catherine de' Medici when she was
six years old. Her bridegroom-to-be was then four
and a half. Mary's education was extensive and her
life in France very happy. Her mother remained in
Scotland as dowager queen under Mary's regency.
So close was Mary to France and things French that
she almost considered herself a Frenchwoman. The

terms of the marriage contract, in fact, practically made Scotland a vassal of France.

The marriage ceremony took place in Notre Dame Cathedral in 1558, when Mary was sixteen, her husband fifteen. She made a radiant and lovely bride. Her hair was a rich chestnut brown, her eyes dark, and her complexion smooth. She was dressed in a white damask robe with a train so long that twenty ladies-in-waiting bore it. Her cloak was of bluish-gray velvet heavily embroidered with white silk and pearls. Her crown was far more costly than any Scottish monarch could boast; it was fashioned of the finest gold and set with diamonds, pearls, rubies, and emeralds.

The customary round of banquets, balls, and pageants followed the marriage ceremony. The French were pleased with the pretty wife of their dauphin, and her young husband, though sickly, adored her. That happiness, however, was soon cut short.

The death of Mary I, queen of England (Mary Tudor), and the accession of twenty-five-year-old Elizabeth to the throne six months later, paved the way for the first fatal step. At a celebration in honor of the marriage of Elizabeth of France to Philip II of Spain, Mary took her place in the royal balcony and was impetuously hailed as the "queen of England" by her father-in-law, King Henry II. As the nobles present took up the cry, they little imagined that they were sounding the death knell of the lovely girl. It was Mary Stuart's assumption of this claim to the English throne occupied by Queen Elizabeth that, twenty-seven years later, cost Mary her life.

At the tournament celebrating this very marriage, Henry II of France met with the jousting accident which caused his death. Mary's husband was then crowned king as Francis II, but less than a year after his coronation, he died and the Scottish queen was left a widow.

Catherine de' Medici, the dowager queen of France, became regent for her son Charles IX, and Mary was relegated to a minor place by her mother-in-law. Since her own mother had died six months before, Mary felt that her place was in her homeland, to which she returned in 1561, when she was eighteen years old.

Mary Stuart's resumption of the Scottish throne was not accomplished easily. Both England and Scotland were torn by the religious differences of the Reformation. Mary, a Catholic in stanchly Protestant Scotland, found herself resented and distrusted by many of her subjects. She attempted to temper John Knox's fiery attack upon her without success; he became more and more virulent and outspoken, declaring that he had no hope that the queen "will ever come to God or do good to the Commonwealth," and she stoutly rejected his public urgings that she forsake "the congregation of Satan," his name for the Roman Catholic Church.

To her religious troubles at home were added political problems with the Protestant Elizabeth of England. As a granddaughter of a sister of Henry VIII, Mary was a formidable claimant to the English throne. She based her claim on that lineage and the fact that Elizabeth had been declared illegitimate by the Pope, and therefore not entitled to the crown. Encouraged by her Catholic supporters Mary urged Elizabeth to name her heir to the throne of England.

At this time Mary might have been able to consolidate her position by a wise marriage. Instead, casting aside the suggestions of her French Catholic relatives, and of Elizabeth, she chose a man who could not fail to damage her cause. Her cousin Henry Stuart, Lord Darnley, had won her by his courtly manners and appearance. Mary called him "the properest and best proportioned long man I have ever seen . . . well instructed for his youth in all honest and comely endeavors." He was a Catholic also, and their marriage in 1565 made her the target of her Protestant enemies, aided and abetted by the machinations of her half brother, James, the earl of Moray. Taking advantage of his desire to overthrow Mary and gain the throne for himself, Elizabeth assigned him to stir up rebellion in Scotland.

Mary made another unfortunate move in choosing

an Italian Catholic, David Rizzio, as her major adviser and personal secretary. Many Protestants regarded him as an emissary of the Pope in Rome. Her
husband, Darnley, proved to be a jealous, immoral
fop, and Mary, soon pregnant, considered the marriage a mistake. In a complete turnabout because
of his suspicion of her infidelity with Rizzio, Darnley
allied himself with the Protestant party which had
opposed his marriage to Mary. One evening in
March, 1566, his agents burst into Mary's apartments
in Edinburgh's Holyrood Palace, dragged Rizzio
out, and stabbed him to death.

Though horrified by this murder, Mary shielded
her husband and helped him escape prosecution.
Two months afterward she gave birth to a son, who
later became James VI of Scotland and James I of
England. During the rest of that year she pretended
devotion to Darnley, but had meanwhile fallen hope-
lessly in love with the married earl of Bothwell, "a
glorious, rash, and hazardous man" she called him.
Together they set the stage for her husband's murder. Seriously ill, Darnley was with his family in
Glasgow, but Mary persuaded him to return to Edinburgh where she could watch over him, and installed
him in Kirk o' Field in the nearby countryside.

On the evening of February 10, 1567, the house
was blown up, and Darnley's body found in the
garden. No marks from the explosion were found

on him and he had apparently been set upon and suffocated. Suspicion quite naturally fell on the queen and Bothwell, and the question of the extent of her knowledge of her husband's murder has never been settled. Outrage at the crime was everywhere expressed. Even her cousin Elizabeth could not contain her anxiety for Mary's future.

"For the love of God, Madam," Elizabeth wrote to Mary, "use sincerity and prudence in this case, which touches you so nearly, that all the world may have reason to judge you innocent of so enormous a crime. Unless you do, you will be worthily blotted out from the rank of princesses and rendered, not undeservedly, the opprobrium of the vulgar, rather than which fate should befall you, I should wish you an honorable sepulchre instead of a stained life."

All Scotland was sure that Bothwell was the murderer. He was formally charged, but since no accusers or witnesses dared to appear against him for fear of reprisals by the queen, he was acquitted. Within three months he was divorced from his wife of one year, and he and Mary were wedded by a Protestant bishop. This indiscretion alienated both Catholics and Protestants, and the Scottish nobles of both faiths banded together against the couple.

Mary and her new consort were unable to raise an army large enough for their defense. On June 15, exactly a month to the day after their wedding, their troops were forced to surrender to the overwhelming numbers of their attackers at Carberry Hill. Bothwell was permitted to escape into exile, and died raving mad in Denmark twelve years later. Mary was made prisoner and forced to abdicate in favor of her baby son. She appealed without success to Elizabeth and Catherine de' Medici. Finally, after ten months' imprisonment, she escaped and rallied a force of six thousand loyal clansmen around her. They were defeated by the royal forces under her half brother, Moray, who had been appointed regent.

Seeking the protection of Queen Elizabeth, Mary fled to England on May 16, 1568. Instead of aiding her cousin in regaining her throne, however, Elizabeth almost completely ignored her. She even refused to meet Mary in person. Because of the growing power of the Protestants in England, Elizabeth would not recognize Mary as queen by pledging her support. She was still fearful of this Catholic claimant to her throne.

The English queen found a way out temporarily by declaring that she could not see Mary or do anything for her until the question of her guilt or innocence as an accomplice in the murder of Darnley had been established. A royal commission therefore began examining the evidence, with Moray as Mary's chief accuser. The findings were inconclusive, but

Mary's reputation suffered, and much of her support was lost.

Now, as one of her biographers has put it, "Instead of a haven, England had proved a trap; instead of a protector, Elizabeth had revealed herself a destroyer." Mary was taken into custody and transferred from prison to prison and castle to castle, each time more closely confined, each day treated with less respect.

For nineteen interminable years Queen Elizabeth continued this "honorable custody" (her term for Mary's unlawful detention), permitting Mary's devoted supporters to plot for her return to the throne of Scotland. Mary received a papal recognition of a divorce from Bothwell, and reaffirmed her loyalty to the Church. Leaders of unsuccessful attempts to rescue her were beheaded. The duke of Norfolk, who had fallen in love with her, was first imprisoned by Elizabeth in the Tower of London, then executed for treason.

Mary's half brother, Moray, was assassinated, but still no genuine support came to her. As her son, James VI of Scotland, grew he became a pensioner of Queen Elizabeth and unsympathetic with the Catholic adherents to his mother's rights. Hence Mary's hopes of ever returning to Scotland were destroyed completely.

As the years passed, the necessity of holding Mary

captive preyed more and more on Elizabeth's mind.
Without her knowledge, Elizabeth's advisers therefore concocted a plot in which Mary was encouraged
to become the leader of a conspiracy against the
English queen, calling for her murder and Mary's
elevation to the English throne. The voluminous and
detailed correspondence, when revealed according
to plan, was completely damning.

Mary was brought to trial and accused of high
treason and "conspiring against the safety of our beloved monarch." Her trial was completely illegal.
No one was allowed to plead for her; she had neither
advocates nor counsel and was not even shown the
letters and documents on which the charges were
founded. She steadfastly denied the right of the
court to try her, demanding to be heard in Parliament and to be permitted to see the queen in person.
All this, of course, was denied her.

After she had been found guilty of treason, Mary
wrote her last letter to Elizabeth. While denying
again all the accusations brought against her, she
made no plea for mercy from the inevitable sentence
of death. Instead she asked that she not be executed
privately lest her enemies say that she had committed suicide and had therefore not received the
last rites of the Catholic Church.

Because she felt that she alone would be held responsible, Elizabeth delayed signing the warrant for execution. Rumor still persists that her ministers, alarmed at her procrastination, arranged for her signature to be forged. In fact, twenty years later, an alleged confession was made public, in which the deceased secretary of one of the ministers admitted the forgery. In any case, the death warrant was signed on February 1, 1587.

When the envoys of Queen Elizabeth arrived at Fotheringhay Castle late on the afternoon of February 7 and announced her sentence, Mary expressed no surprise, merely saying, "I am thankful for such welcome news." After again maintaining her innocence, she asked when her execution would take place, and one of the noblemen replied, "Tomorrow morning at eight o'clock."

Mary Stuart was stunned. "The time," she said, "is very short."

At six o'clock the next morning she dressed in a gown of black satin with purple sleeves and a white veil, her rosary with its golden cross hanging from her belt. When the sheriff arrived, she was permitted to choose six of her attendants to accompany her as witnesses.

Several hundred nobles were assembled in the great hall where her trial had been held, and which was now to be the scene of its resultant sentence. A platform two by twelve feet had been erected in the center. The railings had been draped in black, and on the platform were only a low stool, a cushion, and the block.

As Mary ascended the steps of the scaffold, her last jailer extended his hand to help her. With queenly courtesy she accepted it, saying, "I thank you, sir. This is the last trouble I shall ever give you." The commissioner then read the text of her death warrant and, according to custom, asked if she had anything to say in her defense. She could only repeat briefly that she was innocent and forgave them "with a good heart."

As her two executioners in their black gowns and masks knelt to ask the usual pardon, Mary replied, "I forgive you with all my heart, for now, I hope, this death shall give an end to all my troubles."

When her upper garments had been removed, she stood clothed in a crimson velvet petticoat with bodice and sleeves of the same material, and her eyes were blindfolded by a handkerchief. Mary then knelt upon the cushion and repeated clearly, "In thee, Lord, have I hoped." Bowing her head upon the executioner's block without hesitation, she said in Latin, "Into thy hands, O Lord, I commend my spirit."

The executioner was understandably nervous, and it was not until the third stroke of the axe that the queen's head was severed. As he held the head high for all to see, the commissioner cried, "So perish all Queen Elizabeth's enemies!"

Mary Stuart has rightly been called "the Queen of Paradox." Historians who defend her claim that she was innocent, not only of political connivance for power and to uphold her religion, but of murder as well. Those who denounce her declare that she was guilty of many crimes and a skillful mistress of intrigue.

Perhaps the truth lies midway between these two points of view regarding the ill-starred Queen of Scots who lived out more than half of her forty-four years in prisons.

8

Maria Theresa

1717-1780

The four leading monarchs of Europe in the eighteenth century were Louis XV of France, Frederick the Great of Prussia, Catherine II of Russia, and Maria Theresa of Austria. Of the latter Frederick, though her political and military foe, said, "She was an honor to her sex and the glory of her throne."

When a baby princess was born in the royal palace at Vienna on the thirteenth of May, 1717, her father had difficulty in concealing his disappointment. Charles VI, archduke of Austria, king of Hungary, king of Bohemia, and emperor of the Holy Roman Empire, was the last male representative of his line, the Hapsburgs, and he had hoped that his wife would produce a son to succeed him. The infant was christened Maria Theresa Walburga Amalia Christina, but her last three names were never used.

Though not the son he had prayed for, Maria Theresa was to outshine her illustrious father in strength of character and executive ability. She was intelligent, energetic, and ready in any emergency. She was always conscious of the dignities and duties of her position. Unlike that of many monarchs, her personal conduct was never touched by scandal. She demanded moral and decorous behavior of the members of her court.

Because of her basic honesty and directness, Maria Theresa seldom practiced deceit and cunning in her statesmanship. She stated that in conducting foreign relations during her long rule, she only once had been guilty of "unworthy behavior." This she justified to herself, however, because it achieved the desired result.

The Austrian ambassador to France, Count Kaunitz, had been unable to discuss with King Louis XV a proposed alliance of Austria and France against their common enemy, Emperor Frederick the Great of Prussia. This treaty of friendship was one of Maria Theresa's greatest desires, and she decided to take matters into her own hands. Madame de Pompadour, Louis' mistress and the real ruler of France, was the key to the monarch's attention. So, though she felt it beneath her royal dignity to deal with both a courtesan and a commoner, Maria Theresa put aside her prejudices. She began a regular and friendly correspondence with Madame de Pompadour, at first full of personal salutations and exchanges of minor court gossip. This produced the desired effect. Madame de Pompadour was so flattered by such a mark of attention from the great empress that she became Maria Theresa's intermediary with the king in promoting the alliance proposal. The lengthy correspondence continued, with the empress briefing the courtesan with arguments and answers to Louis' objections. Madame de Pompadour finally convinced the king that alliance with Austria was in the best interests of France.

In 1736, when she was nineteen, Maria Theresa was married to her cousin, Francis, duke of Lorraine. The marriage was based on love rather than politics, and the union was a happy one. Francis lacked the quick, capable mind of his wife, but Maria Theresa's affection for him was constant through the more than twenty-nine years of their marriage.

The death of her father, Charles VI, left Maria Theresa, at twenty-three, queen of Hungary, queen of Bohemia, archduchess of Austria, sovereign of the Netherlands, and duchess of Milan, Parma, and Piacenza. Through her husband she was also grand duchess of Tuscany. Despite these impressive titles, her situation at that time was desperate. She had, however, prepared herself for the duties of a ruler.

Her father had attempted to secure her undisputed succession by means of the Pragmatic Sanction, which declared, in the absence of a male heir, that Maria Theresa was heiress of the possessions of the Austrian Hapsburgs. These included Austria itself, Bohemia, Hungary, Lombardy, and a large part of the Netherlands. This declaration had been ratified by the major European powers, but dissension arose from all directions as soon as Charles VI was dead.

The first official act of the new monarch was to ask for recognition of her government. Within the first few months of Maria Theresa's reign the Pragmatic Sanction was completely ignored. France at first postponed an answer, then declined to acknowledge her title. Charles of Bavaria, supported by France, claimed Austria, Hungary, and Bohemia. The king of Spain put in his bid for the Austrian succession and prepared to seize the Italian states. The king of Sardinia claimed Milan. Frederick the Great seized the duchy of Silesia, which he laid waste and occupied with his armies.

The perils which confronted the young queen at her accession would have overwhelmed a less determined woman. Maria Theresa was surrounded by enemies and threatened from within. She was without an army, without a treasury, and without a ministry, for those who composed her council of state agreed on only one thing—their jealousy of the influence of the duke of Lorraine, her husband.

Maria Theresa, however, was never more effective than in adversity, and her courageous statecraft now came to her aid. Hungary clung firmly to its dauntless queen, and it was to Hungary that she turned for help, promising it a measure of self-government.

On June 25, 1741, she was crowned queen of Hungary at Pressburg, the capital of Hungary at that time. The iron crown of St. Stephen was placed on her head, his shield in her left hand. Over her royal robes was draped his tattered mantle, the emblem of Hungarian authority. Mounted on a black stallion, she galloped up the Royal Mount, a hill near Pressburg, and at its summit, following ancient custom, she drew forth the glistening sword of St. Stephen and waved it around her head, symbolizing her defiance of the four corners of the world.

Three months later, when an army of French and Bavarians invaded Bohemia, Maria Theresa appeared before the Hungarian Assembly to appeal for the country's help in saving her crown and her house from ruin. She called upon their patriotism, emphasizing her helpless condition as queen, woman, and mother. As she committed herself and her children to the fidelity of her subjects and lifted her infant son Joseph in her arms, a thousand warriors drew their swords and shouted, "We will die for our queen Maria Theresa!" The Assembly voted to put 100,000 soldiers in the field immediately.

The fame of her heroic stand spread to England. There the plight of this young and fiery queen excited sympathy. Parliament voted 300,000 pounds to support her in her struggle.

Enthusiasm for her cause spread throughout her kingdom, and bands of soldiers flocked to her aid. She fortified her capital, Vienna, while Prussia looked on in astonishment. To avoid an attack by Frederick the Great, Maria Theresa was forced to cede Silesia to him.

Charles of Bavaria seized Prague, the capital of Bohemia, and was crowned emperor of Germany with the title of Charles VII. But within a few months the Bavarians and the French were defeated, and Maria Theresa reentered Prague. She was crowned queen of Bohemia there in May, 1743. She was also victorious in Italy. Charles VII died soon after, and Maria Theresa was able to fulfill her ambition of placing the imperial crown upon her husband's head. Francis was proclaimed emperor of Germany at Frankfurt in September, 1745, and Maria Theresa was the first to exclaim, "Long live the Emperor Francis I!"

By 1748 Maria Theresa had regained possession of all her inheritance except Silesia, Parma, and Piacenza. She had also obtained guarantee of the Pragmatic Sanction from the principal European powers. Her father had left her with an empty treasury, but even after eight years of war (called the War of Austrian Succession), her revenues, because of careful management, exceeded those of her predecessors by six million florins. And all this was while she was still a young woman!

As soon as a peace treaty was signed, Maria Theresa introduced a program of internal reforms, which was designed to build a united nation from her realms. Her term for this project was benevolent monarchism, by which she meant a strong central government devoted to the welfare of its subjects and thoroughly worthy of their support. She overhauled the taxation system to require payment from both the nobility and the clergy, established crown courts, and built up a national army. Special encouragement was given to agriculture, industry, commerce, and the arts. Education became a responsibility of the state rather than the church. Public high schools and lower schools were established. During this period of peace, the countries that made up the Austrian empire were united as never before, under Maria Theresa, the only woman ruler in the long Hapsburg dynasty.

Austria's second major conflict with Frederick the Great, the Seven Years' War (1756–1763), brought only a terrific loss of life and money to both sides. Not a foot of territory was gained or lost by either party. At the war's end Maria Theresa was forty-six years of age. For twenty-three years of her reign all Europe had watched her with wonder and admiration. Fourteen of these years had been spent in war. Now she wanted to continue her internal reforms and plan for the future.

Maria Theresa well deserved the title of "mother of her people," by which she was long known. She was always ready to sacrifice herself for the good of her realm. "I reproach myself," she once said, "with the time I spend in sleep as so much robbed from my people."

She was proud of her reputation as a benefactor. She founded hospitals for sick and wounded soldiers and homes for army officers' widows and young women of poor families. With such a belligerent neighbor as Frederick the Great, she could never be sure of continued peace, and therefore she maintained a large army of disciplined troops and established military academies at Vienna, Neustadt, and Antwerp. Even her enemy Frederick the Great was impressed, acknowledging that "the Austrian army acquired, under the auspices of Maria Theresa, such a degree of perfection as it had never attained under any of her predecessors, and a woman accomplished designs worthy of a great man."

In 1767, about two years after the death of her husband, Maria Theresa became a victim of smallpox and her face was badly scarred. This disease had been a scourge of the Hapsburgs, killing three of her daughters and two daughters-in-law and scarring three other daughters with hideous pockmarks. Under her supervision the royal physicians established an experimental smallpox hospital and clinic in Vienna, and finally succeeded in developing an inoculation against the disease.

During these years of peace, Maria Theresa lived simply, spending her days attending to affairs of state and her evenings with her children. A devout Catholic, she always held prayers with them before retiring.

Maria Theresa's record of motherhood is probably not matched by any other great queen in history. Five sons and eleven daughters were born to the Austrian queen within twenty years. In the midst of her strenuous duties, she found time to supervise their care and education. Her children returned their mother's devotion.

Six children, one son and five daughters, died either in infancy or before reaching their mid-teens. As the others grew up and took their place in the world, they all proved a credit to their mother.

When Francis I died in 1765, the eldest son, twenty-four-year-old Joseph became coregent with his mother as Emperor Joseph II. Leopold was grand duke of Tuscany for twenty-five years before succeeding Joseph in 1790. Ferdinand married the heiress of the house of Modena, becoming the duke of Modena. Maximilian became elector of Cologne.

Four of the daughters were attractive and accomplished, and Maria Theresa proved herself a good matchmaker. Marie Antoinette became the wife of Louis XVI and queen of France. Christina, the favorite, married Prince Albert of Saxony. Like her mother's, this union was for love rather than for political expediency. Amalia married the duke of Parma, Caroline the king of Naples. Two less personable sisters, sickly Marianna and horribly pockmarked Elizabeth, took church vows and became abbesses.

When war with Prussia threatened once again, Maria Theresa's skillful negotiations were able to prevent it. This peace in 1779 was concluded without either battle or bloodshed, and she declared that no event of her long reign gave her such satisfaction as this last diplomatic success.

On the last night of her life Maria Theresa was engaged in signing papers and giving detailed instructions to her son Joseph, who was to succeed her. When he urged her to rest, she answered, "In a few hours I shall be gone. Would you have me spend them in sleep?"

Thus Maria Theresa died on November 29, 1780, when she was sixty-three, after having reigned for forty years. Her chief accomplishment was holding the Austrian empire together against the territorial ambitions of Frederick the Great in central Europe. This queen's almost matchless skill in statesmanship and politics, her wise choice of advisers, and above all her selfless devotion to her kingdom, have led her to be called "the most beneficent sovereign who ever wore a crown." She has gone down in history as one of the greatest queens who ever lived, and in the lands which she governed her memory is revered to this day.

9

Catherine II of Russia

1729-1796

The importance of Catherine the Great lay in her accomplishments for her adopted country, Russia. Through her political acumen and adroit statesmanship, she enlarged its dominions and made it one of the leading European powers in the eighteenth century. Before her rule, Russia had been a semiprimitive country, more Asiatic than European. Continuing the work of Peter the Great, which had been interrupted for almost forty years after his death, Catherine brought culture and a touch of the civilization of the West to the nation and people she learned to love.

About May 2, 1729—Catherine never knew the exact date—at Stettin in Prussia, the wife of an army general gave birth to a daughter. The mother, Johanna Elizabeth, was a princess of the Romanov family, the royal line of Russia; the father was a minor prince of a small Prussian state. The infant was named Sophia Augusta Frederica and bore the title princess of Anhalt-Zerbst. In spite of her noble lineage, however, her childhood was passed in stern and drab surroundings.

In 1741 Princess Johanna received an invitation from Empress Elizabeth of Russia to bring her daughter to St. Petersburg for "a long visit." Though not definitely stated, the purpose of the visit was the betrothal of fifteen-year-old Sophia to Peter, the nephew of the empress. Elizabeth had brought him to the Russian capital from one of the Prussian states, given him the title of grand duke, and designated him as her heir. Sophia had met Peter once when he was eleven, and remembered him as being ugly, with hideous smallpox scars, and possessed of an unpleasant disposition. But personal feelings and wishes were never considered in such arranged marriages.

Princess Sophia's life in the capital was a complete contrast to her girlhood. St. Petersburg, now called Leningrad, had been founded forty years before by Peter the Great to replace Moscow as the seat of government. It was a beautiful city of palaces, gardens, and wide boulevards. At the court the young girl was surrounded by a magnificence beyond her wildest dreams, but she soon discovered that court life involved continuous intrigues, plots, and counterplots.

Sophia's future aunt-in-law, Empress Elizabeth, had gained her throne in 1741 by imprisoning the year-old Tsar Ivan and banishing his mother, the regent, from Russia. Throughout her rule of twenty years she was to prove a despot, and her actions were an example to Sophia of all that was bad in a monarch.

The prospective bride was trained for her future position as wife of the ruler of Russia. She said later that her trials before and after her marriage were made bearable only by her dreams of power. "I did not care about Peter," she wrote, "but I did about the crown." She determined to become a Russian. First she was converted from Lutheranism to the Greek Orthodox Church, the state religion, and adopted the name of Catherine Alexeievna. She made this transition without scruples as a part of her training to become empress. Catherine then began studying the Russian language and the history of her adopted nation.

When the day of the marriage arrived, on the twenty-first of August, 1745, both sixteen-year-old Catherine and Peter, a year older, accepted the fact that the alliance was loveless. Though he was destined for the throne, Peter made no attempt to interest himself in the problems of Russia. He continued to think of himself as Prussian. Peter was dissolute and weak, almost childish, and unintelligent (some said feeble-minded) as well as physically unattractive.

Catherine had difficulty in concealing her loathing for her husband. Throughout the years of her marriage and after, Catherine had many love affairs with attractive and stimulating men. During her reign some of these favorites were advanced beyond their capabilities, while others proved valuable advisers and aides to the empress.

In order to fit herself for the future, Catherine, now grand duchess of Russia, set about gaining the confidence of Empress Elizabeth. In addition to her interest in affairs of state, she began to find joy in books, a taste which remained with her throughout her life.

During her apprenticeship, Catherine's knowledge of the country and government developed so completely that she very early resolved to seize the Russian throne for herself upon the death of the empress. She made no pretense of happiness in her marriage, but a son, Paul, born in 1754, was accepted as legitimate, though not designated as Peter's heir by the empress. When Elizabeth died in January of 1762, Peter became Peter III.

The new emperor's incompetence and offensive behavior were so apparent that his wife had to wait only six months before seizing the throne. Peter III drew up a treaty of alliance with Frederick the Great. of Prussia, who had been the bitterest of Russia's enemies during the Seven Years' War. He insulted Catherine publicly and threatened to replace her by his mistress. He postponed the formal coronation ceremony. Meanwhile Catherine, in conspiracy with the noble and powerful Orlov family, carefully plotted a bloodless revolution.

On the evening of the eighth of July, 1762, Catherine was at Peterhof Palace, nineteen miles from St. Petersburg. Peter was to arrive from Oranienbaum, another country house, the next day for the celebration of his name-day. The emperor's troops were assembled in the capital, ready to leave for a campaign against Denmark. But through the machinations of the five Orlov brothers, several regiments had been prepared to mutiny against their commander-in-chief.

At six o'clock on the morning of the ninth, one of the brothers awakened Catherine. The time was at hand, the moment of action must be seized immediately. After a breakneck race to St. Petersburg, the empress went from regiment to regiment, telling the soldiers that her husband intended to kill her that very night, and that they were her only protection.

They believed her, and swore to die, if necessary, in her defense. The officers raised the cry of "Long live the Empress Catherine!" and the soldiers echoed the shout.

In a grand procession they followed her to the cathedral, where many of the nobles and clergy of the church were assembled. The archbishop of Novgorod proclaimed her as the ruler of Russia, with her eight-year-old son, Grand Duke Paul, as her heir and successor. Within two hours Catherine had placed herself upon the throne, with an army at her command and the capital at her feet.

The royal entourage then went to the Winter Palace, where a long-prepared manifesto was read, claiming that this act was necessary to save the throne from Prussia and the official church from being supplanted by Lutheranism. When Catherine appeared on a balcony with her son, the victory was hers. Thousands of her soldiers and subjects were allowed to tramp through the palace and kiss the hand of their new empress.

Peter III knew nothing of the events in St. Petersburg. When he arrived at the Peterhof Palace for the name-day celebration, he learned of his wife's treachery from the peasant who brought the fireworks from the capital. In a panic he returned to Oranienbaum to confer with his advisers. At ten o'clock on the night of that decisive June day, Catherine, who had assumed the title of colonel of the Royal Guard, donned a uniform, and mounted a white horse. Heading a cavalcade of fourteen thousand of her troops, she rode to Peterhof with the intention of seizing Peter. Since he was no longer there, Catherine dispatched a representative to Oranienbaum, and her husband was "persuaded" to sign a declaration that he had voluntarily abdicated. Peter was then taken prisoner and placed under guard in the palace of Ropsha near St. Petersburg.

Now securely in control, Catherine II began to consider how she could best retain her newly acquired power. First of all Peter III must be disposed of. Accordingly, he was strangled nine days later, probably by Catherine's followers. On the next day his death was formally announced, the empress issuing a manifesto stating that it had "pleased Almighty God to remove the late emperor from this world by a violent malady." Although no one believed this statement, no one was bold enough to contradict it.

As a sovereign, Catherine the Great displayed marked ability in leadership. She was astute in judgment, shrewd in action, and hard and ruthless. She set about making Russia a first-class power. Frederick the Great of Prussia, Louis XV of France, Maria Theresa of Austria, and George III of England, each in his turn, learned to be wary of her actions.

The first of her ambitious objectives was to extend her empire. She began with Poland. Both Russia to the east and Prussia to the west coveted the provinces adjoining their frontiers. The Polish crown was elective rather than hereditary, and Catherine, in league with Frederick the Great, acted swiftly when King Augustus III died in 1763. When the Polish nobles failed to agree on a successor, Catherine put forth her own candidate, a former favorite of hers who was of Polish ancestry. He was duly elected. But soon the country was torn with a religious dispute and a surge of nationalism. Taking advantage of this situation, Catherine sent her troops to protect her puppet king, put down the rebellion, and dictate the laws.

When Poland continued to prove incapable of governing itself, Catherine partitioned parts of the country among Russia, Prussia, and Austria in 1772. In 1793 she seized additional territory, this time sharing only with Prussia. When another independence movement, led by the patriot Kosciuszko, was put down, a third partition in 1795 wiped Poland from the map. Within a little over two decades, largely through the machinations of its empress, Russia had also gained Lithuania and a large part of the Ukraine.

Another of Catherine's dreams was to extend the southern borders of her kingdom to the Black Sea. Following several years of war against Turkey, ending in 1774, Russia annexed the whole northern shore line of the Black Sea except Crimea, which she added nine years later. The treaty following a second war, in which the imperial army was led by Potemkin against the combined Turko-Swedish forces, made the possession of the Black Sea steppes and Crimea official in 1792.

Russia was also permitted free navigation of the Black Sea. When its ships could pass freely past Constantinople through the Bosporus, Russian trade was extended to the Mediterranean and thus to the countries of western Europe.

Catherine was also responsible for Russia's colonization of Alaska and its monopoly of the rich fur trade. Before her reign the government had sponsored several expeditions to explore the Aleutian Islands. But in 1784 Catherine sent a rich fur merchant, Shelekhov, sometimes called the "Russian Columbus," to found the first permanent settlement in Alaska on Kodiak Island. Other expeditions penetrated the Alaskan Peninsula, and eventually Russian merchants organized the fur trade that had previously been carried on by individual Siberian hunters. These merchants were consolidated in 1788 into a single company, and by royal charter enjoyed a monopoly of the fur trade throughout the entire region.

During her long reign, while she was making her

country powerful, Catherine the Great did not neglect the internal affairs of Russia. She appointed a commission of both nobles and peasants to codify the existing laws, which were favorable to the nobility. The effects of these deliberations, however, were not felt until long after her death. Serfdom flourished, and the peasants had few rights during her reign. Because of Catherine's dependence upon the serf-owning class, she could only make suggestions regarding the reduction or elimination of bondage.

The empress developed a network of provincial schools which emphasized maternal care and child welfare. Catherine doubled the resources and revenues of her empire by shrewd administration of her conquered territories and by a revision of the internal tax structure. At about the same time as Maria Theresa in Austria, she introduced inoculation against smallpox, the scourge of the eighteenth century, throughout her empire.

Because of Russia's traditional isolation from western Europe, Catherine's predecessors had paid little attention to cultural development. The empress made up for this lack by becoming a patron of literature and the fine arts. She surrounded herself with men of letters, and especially cultivated the friendship of French writers. She purchased vast book collections and brought them to St. Petersburg. She added an Italian opera company to her establishment. In the gallery of the Hermitage, which she built next to the Winter Palace, she hung fine specimens of the Italian and Flemish schools of painting, forming an outstanding collection which has survived to the present.

Catherine II held the reins of government strongly in her hands. Any sign of rebellion was met with force. She was always in full control. Her wishes were law. She was never close to her son, Paul, for whom she acted as regent before he reached his legal majority of eighteen years in 1772. Thereafter his mother dominated his life, keeping him completely in the background. His first wife in a marriage arranged by Catherine died in childbirth. But in less than a year he remarried, and this time two sons, Alexander and Constantine, were born. Catherine began to think of her elder grandson, Alexander, as her successor instead of her son, but never actually so designated him.

The last years of Catherine's reign were filled with frustrations. She seemed unable to impose her will on others as she had so long done. Her final defeat came in September, 1796. Catherine had arranged a marriage between Paul's daughter Alexandrina, then only fifteen years old, and seventeen-year-old King Gustavus Adolphus of Sweden, an alliance she had long desired.

She invited the young monarch and his advisers

to St. Petersburg to draw up and sign the contract.
Catherine had stipulated that the bride-to-be should
be allowed to remain in the Greek Orthodox faith,
in spite of the fact that it was a law of Sweden that
the queen of the country must profess the Lutheran
faith. In her assurance that her granddaughter would
be made an exception to this law, Catherine over-
estimated both her powers of persuasion and the
will of the Swedish monarch. Even so, all the terms
of the contract appeared to be acceptable.

On the evening when the formal ceremony of the
signing was to take place, all the court assembled in
the throne room. Catherine sat on the throne, wearing her royal robes and her diamond crown, with the
Princess Alexandrina beside her. The hour for the
appearance of the Swedish suitor struck, but he did
not arrive. As the minutes, which seemed like years
to the empress and her granddaughter, passed, the
room began to buzz with uneasy whisperings.

At last the diplomat who had drawn up the contract appeared and whispered something into the
ear of the empress. Controlling herself with a mighty
effort, Catherine arose and dismissed the court under
the pretext that the king of Sweden was indisposed.
When she reached her apartment, she fell to the floor
unconscious, in what was probably a mild paralytic
stroke. When she came to she was told that Gustavus
Adolphus would not sign the marriage contract as

long as it contained the clause which permitted Alexandrina to retain the Russian religion.

But the empress, unused to being opposed, would not change her mind. She was consumed with anger that her plan had been thwarted, and this failure seemed to have affected her health. She swore vengeance on the young king, who returned to Sweden a few days later.

Catherine was actually preparing for war with Sweden when, on the seventeenth of November, 1796, she collapsed in an apoplectic stroke and died the next day.

She was sixty-seven years old and had ruled Russia for thirty-four years.

After her death her son, who succeeded to the throne as Paul I, found an inscription she had drawn up for her grave:

Here lies
CATHERINE THE SECOND
born in Stettin on April 21/May 2, 1729
In the year 1744 she went to Russia to marry Peter III. At the age of fifteen she made a three-part resolution: to please her husband, her empress, and the nation.

She neglected nothing in order to succeed in this.

Eighteen years of tedium and solitude caused her to read many books.

When she came to the throne she wished to do good, and strove to introduce happiness, freedom, and prosperity.

She forgave easily and hated no one.

She was good-natured and easy-going. She was cheerful and her heart was kind.

She had friends.

Work came easy to her. She loved sociability and the arts.

This self-eulogy was accurate only in part. Catherine undoubtedly had good intentions, and no monarch ever worked more resolutely for the good of her kingdom—that is, what she thought was its good. Most of her endeavors bore the stamp of her excessive ambition and indomitable will. She spared nothing to gain her ends.

As an absolute monarch unequaled by few rulers in history, Catherine II of Russia well deserves the adjective by which she is always known—the Great.

10

Marie Antoinette

1755-1793

From time to time in the history of nations persons of mediocre character or ability come into power. Sometimes they may be monarchs who are unable to carry out their duties in times of crisis. Occasionally they are queens who become the victims of circumstances.

Marie Antoinette, queen of France during one of its most turbulent and crucial periods, was such a person. She unwittingly became the typical figure of selfish, extravagant, and inefficient royalty. Fate placed her in a role which, considering the weaknesses of her character, could end only in tragedy.

The youngest daughter of Empress Maria Theresa of Austria, she was born in Vienna on the second of

November, 1755, and named Maria Antonia. In 1769 she was betrothed to Louis, the dauphin of France. The next year, when she was not yet fifteen years old, she made the long journey overland to Paris to meet her prospective husband for the first time. She never again saw her homeland.

At the German-French border she discarded her Austrian wardrobe, said good-bye to her attendants, and put on clothes from Paris to enter her new home. Marie Antoinette, as she then became, met her future father-in-law and her seventeen-year-old fiancé at the château of Compiègne. On the sixteenth of May they were married in the chapel of the royal palace at Versailles. Although the royal exchequer was as usual almost empty, twenty million francs, a tremendous sum for that period, was spent on the celebrations which followed.

Four years later King Louis XV died, and cries of "The king is dead! Long live the king!" rang throughout France. The dauphin and his wife fell upon their knees, exclaiming, "Oh, God, guide us, protect us. We are too young to govern!"

A momentous crisis faced France when Louis XVI and Marie Antoinette ascended the throne. The time had arrived when the abuses of the old regime could no longer be tolerated by the people, and sweeping reforms were demanded. If sincerely wishing to see his people prosperous and happy could have made them so, Louis XVI would have been France's most beneficent ruler. But his utter lack of energy and ability to carry out his good intentions soon became all too apparent.

The queen, on the other hand, must certainly have inherited some of her mother's capabilities and strong qualities. Had Louis called upon her for advice and assistance, she might have developed into a helpful consort instead of a foolish woman.

On June 10, 1774, at the cathedral of Rheims, "good Louis XVI," as his subjects called him, was crowned with all the splendor France knew so well how to exhibit. And for a time the people regarded the young monarch as the hope of the nation.

Reared in the informality of the Austrian court, Marie Antoinette found it difficult to adjust to the glittering atmosphere of Versailles. Service to the king and queen was regarded as an honor, and the queen could not pass from one apartment to another without being followed by the lords and ladies of her retinue. She enjoyed no privacy whatsoever, and her life was restricted by protocol.

"How disagreeable! How tiresome!" exclaimed the queen, and so her husband gave her the small country house, Le Petit Trianon. The gift of a place of her own where she could escape from the boring life of the royal court delighted her.

She gathered a lively circle of friends about her

and her freedom from restraint shocked the court. Stories of the irregular behavior of the queen began to circulate throughout France. The king's three maiden aunts lost no opportunity to spread gossip unfavorable to Marie Antoinette. But apparently she did not care. She continued her extravagances, which soon approached the stage of a national scandal. She gambled recklessly and constantly sought new entertainments and pleasures. As her enemies—and she had many—eagerly spread stories and half-truths regarding her conduct, she began to be referred to, disrespectfully, as "the Austrian."

Marie Antoinette was certainly imprudent, but that was her only weakness. At the age of nineteen she had been made first lady in perhaps the most extravagant and lavish court in Europe. The people had begun to compute the cost of palaces, crown jewels, and courtiers, but their queen failed to realize that public opinion was of great importance to her. The right of the common people to judge her amusements was something she could not understand, and therein lay the reason for her later downfall.

Her unpopularity grew. She was the object of both suspicion and dislike. Even the birth of a daughter in 1778 had no effect in improving the public image of her as a feather-brained girl who loved only pleasure. On the twenty-second of October, 1781, a second child and first son was born to Marie Antoinette at Versailles. The nation as well as the king was overjoyed at the birth of an heir to the throne, and criticism of the queen abated for a short time. This child lived only until 1789, but a second son, the dauphin Louis, was born in 1785. Another daughter was born in 1786 and died the following year. Throughout this period, however, the stories of Marie Antoinette's dissolute conduct and reckless spending continued. She became a subject of lampoons which were freely printed and distributed, and was said to have had many lovers.

Nothing damaged her reputation more than the affair of the diamond necklace in 1783–1785. Countess de Lamotte, an adventuress, persuaded Cardinal de Rohan that he would gain Marie Antoinette's favor by purchasing on her behalf a necklace of 647 diamonds costing 1,600,000 livres (the sum of $3,-360,000 today). The cardinal delivered the necklace in darkness to a conspirator impersonating the queen. When the jeweler sought to collect from her the money due him, Marie Antoinette realized that she had unknowingly been used in a gigantic swindle. In spite of her assertion that she knew nothing of the transaction, most Frenchmen believed her guilty of this outlandish expenditure. She was never to live down the episode.

Marie Antoinette had become a detested symbol

of the nobility, and the royal family were to be the most prominent victims of the wrath of their subjects.

On the fifth of May, 1789, a meeting of the States General, or parliament of the people, took place at Versailles. The event was greeted as the dawn of national liberty. But as the procession of delegates wound its way along the streets, the common people observed with mounting displeasure the distinctions of rank and costume which divided their representatives from the nobles and the clergy. Marie Antoinette was greeted not with the usual loud, loyal shouts of "Long live the queen!" but with new, insulting cries. The monarchy and the luxury of the court were attacked in speeches, and the members of the Third Estate (the lower body) applauded loudly.

The nobles watched with jealous eyes the growing power of the common people, and decided that something should be done to extinguish this new spark of liberty. Soon after, the Third Estate declared itself to be the National Assembly, and not subject to the call of the king. During the last week of June, King Louis held an audience of nobles at Versailles. The decision that the nobility had determined to crush the National Assembly was read by the keeper of the seals. Rumors spread that this was to be the beginning of extensive persecution, and that all citizen-patriots were to be massacred.

The fuse of the French Revolution was lighted on July 14, 1789. All Paris was in an uproar. Mobs ransacked the city looking for arms. Swords, pistols, and muskets were taken from private homes. At Versailles the head of the army remained calm, for under his command were fifty thousand troops well armed and equipped. Upon the Champs de Mars, another officer had assembled his force of several thousand Swiss and German mercenaries. At a moment's notice this force could move, in the king's name, on the city of Paris to chastise the rebellious subjects. The enormous fortress of the Bastille also protected the city.

Could the Bastille be taken? the people asked. Suddenly a rumor spread through the mob that there were arms at the Hôtel des Invalides, and there the crowd proceeded. Upon the esplanade of the palace, thirty thousand soldiers stood grim and menacing, but offered no resistance. The gates were thrown open and the crowd poured in to find thirty thousand muskets and six cannon. Then, with one accord, they shouted, "La Bastille! La Bastille!" and rushed out to storm the fortress.

Confusion and bloodshed resulted as priests, nobles, beggars, and wealthy citizens mingled in the assault. Apparently all Paris was united against the monarchy. De Launey, commander of the Bastille, was in despair. The troops from Versailles had not arrived and three-fourths of his own garrison had abandoned him and gone over to the side of the people. Death seemed inevitable.

Finally, after five hours of attack, the white flag of truce was raised from the tower. The firing ceased, and the cry echoed along the streets of Paris: "The Bastille surrenders!" July 14, Bastille Day, is still a national holiday in France today.

The people were now thoroughly aroused, and it was only a question of time before action would be taken against the monarch himself. On the morning of October 5, the hungry populace was in the streets crying for bread. "To Versailles, the land of feasting and plenty!" they cried. Courtiers warned the king of the approaching danger, and he was urged to leave the palace and seek refuge elsewhere. But he was, as usual, irresolute. He decided to await the course of events, not from courage to face whatever might happen, but for want of courage to depart.

In this hour of peril, the queen summoned her hitherto untapped strength of character and will, and met the situation with courage, calm, and firm resolve. Without hesitation, she decided to remain with her husband and her children.

The next morning, October 6, 1789, the multitude, still threatening the palace, demanded that the king return with them to Paris. As he had little choice, he decided to comply. Loud shouts then were raised of *"Vive le roi!"* But threatening voices added, "Down with the Austrian!"

"Madame," said General de Lafayette, who was head of the National Guard, "the king goes to Paris. What will you do?"

"Accompany the king," replied Marie Antoinette promptly.

For nine months of insult and humiliation the royal family remained in the Tuileries palace as virtual prisoners. Finally the king began seriously to contemplate flight; he felt that he might be able to rally his loyal subjects on the frontiers of France, and there try to cope with the difficulties which troubled the kingdom.

Honoré Gabriel de Mirabeau was one of the most powerful figures during the French Revolution. In addition, he was probably the ugliest man and the most persuasive orator in all France. Marie Antoinette believed that he and only he might yet save the monarchy. She therefore arranged to meet him at St. Cloud in July of 1790. The interview lasted less than an hour, and he promised to use his influence on her behalf. "Madame," he said, kissing her hand, "the monarchy is saved!"

But the opportunity to keep or break his pledge was never given to Mirabeau. He died in April, 1791, and his death brought to an end the hopes of the king and queen. Flight now seemed the only course of action.

On the twentieth of June, Louis XVI, Marie Antoinette, the two children, and their governess quietly left the Tuileries under cover of darkness. They entered their waiting carriages and drove rapidly away. But at Varennes the royal family was recognized, arrested, and brought back to Paris, while threats and torrents of abuse were hurled at them by crowds along the way. A forest of glittering bayonets surrounded them when, by the glaring light of torches, they climbed the marble staircase of the Tuileries palace once more.

A year passed by, and with each turbulent day the safety of the royal family became more and more precarious. On the advice of his counselors, Louis decided to appeal in person to the National Assembly. The hall was packed with people and the silence which greeted the appearance of the king was menacing. The king chose this moment to whisper to an attendant. A few of the deputies were fearful that he was summoning some of the guards who might have been bribed to spirit him away.

"What order has the king given?" one asked of the attendant.

"Why, my friends," replied the laughing attendant, "do you not know you are dealing with a Bourbon? The king has simply *ordered his dinner!*"

And so, in the midst of the National Assembly, while a raging mob was storming the Tuileries, and his good Swiss guards were pouring out their lifeblood in its defense upon the marble stairs, and the throne of his ancestors was tottering in the balance, King Louis munched his bread and drank his wine. He never really understood the seriousness of his situation.

Now followed long months of imprisonment in the Temple, while the king was on trial for his life. Then came the sorrowful night of January 20, 1793, when for the last time Louis XVI was permitted to see his family. The next morning he died upon the guillotine.

The queen remained in prison until August, when she was taken from her children and moved to the Conciergerie, the common prison. She was led down the steps of a damp dungeon and thrust into a barricaded cell. A candle gave her just light enough to reveal its horrors. The floor was covered with mud. A bundle of straw with a coarse and tattered covering served as her bed. There was a small pine table and a single chair.

Here for two long, weary months Marie Antoinette suffered every deprivation and humiliation.

Everything was taken from her—a watch her mother had given her in Vienna, her mementoes of her children. On the fourteenth of October she was summoned to appear before the judges. She stood before them, a frail woman in a tattered black dress.

The act of accusation was read and the witnesses appeared. There were forty-one—men of all sorts and conditions of life, ready to swear anything, however atrocious, against the queen.

Marie Antoinette endured the trial for twenty long hours, listening apparently unmoved to the accusations against her and finally to the sentence of her death. She was to die on the guillotine two days later.

At last the trial was over, and the queen was asked if she had anything to say. She lifted her head proudly and answered:

"I was a queen, and you took away my crown; a wife, you killed my husband; a mother, and you deprived me of my children. My blood alone remains. Take it, but do not make me suffer long." Then rising from her seat, she walked calmly away. She was thirty-eight, and had been twenty-three years in France.

All Paris was under arms on the morning of October 16, 1793. Thirty thousand troops lined the route of the queen's passage. The bridges were guarded with cannon.

Before the prison, where the crowd was thickest,

stood a wretched cart with a single horse, a plank the only seat. A moment later Marie Antoinette stepped into the open cart. Slowly the cart wound its way through the streets, while the crowds yelled, shouted, and mocked the silent, white-robed figure.

At last the cart drew up at the foot of the scaffold. The queen mounted the steps and, kneeling, uttered a brief prayer, then turning her eyes to the distant towers of the Temple, she exclaimed, "Adieu, my children. I go to rejoin your father."

She was bound to the plank. The gleaming axe slid into the groove, and the lovely Austrian, who had never willingly harmed a living soul, was beheaded. The tragedy of the life of Marie Antoinette was finished.

11

Josephine

1763-1814

The facts of history are often stranger than fiction, and among the characters of poetry and romance there are few whose stories are as unusual as that of Josephine, the Creole beauty of simple background who became the wife of Napoleon Bonaparte and empress of France.

Josephine, the daughter of Joseph Tascher, lieutenant in the coast artillery and a sugar planter, was born on the island of Martinique in the French West Indies. When she was sixteen she was betrothed to the Viscount Alexandre de Beauharnais, whom she had not seen since childhood. The nineteen-year-old son of a former governor of Martinique, he lived in Paris, and the arrangements were made by mail.

After their marriage in a suburb of Paris, the couple soon discovered that the differences in their backgrounds—she the somewhat unsophisticated country girl, he the aristocratic dandy—made them incompatible. Though they had two children, Eugene and Hortense, during the four years they were together, they decided to separate. The viscountess Josephine de Beauharnais set about acquiring the necessary social graces, returning to Martinique for a two-year visit in 1788. When she went back to Paris the Revolution was beginning in France. Josephine pleaded for a reconciliation with her husband, but the couple continued to live apart.

Alexandre had become prominent in the turbulent politics of France. Though an aristocrat, he began to express sympathies for the people, calling himself Citizen Beauharnais. He was even elected president of the Constituent Assembly. But in the chaos following the execution of King Louis XVI and Queen Marie Antoinette, his aristocratic birth was remembered and he was guillotined in 1794. Josephine was arrested and imprisoned for several months, but the fall of Robespierre and the end of the Revolution saved her, and she was freed.

Though dependent on loans from her mother and friends, the thirty-one-year-old widow lived extravagantly. Hortense was sent to a private school, Eugene to a military academy. Very soon Josephine be-

came acquainted with an artillery major in the
French army named Napoleon Bonaparte, but paid
little attention to him, for he was six years younger
and three inches shorter than she. When he was
promoted to general, however, the ambitious widow
was impressed and set out to capture him. Capital-
izing on his excessive shyness and his lack of experience with women, she flattered and praised him.
Soon he was her devoted slave, determined to marry
her. He talked freely of his ambitions and begged
her to share the road to greatness with him.

After Josephine de Beauharnais became engaged
to General Bonaparte, she took him with her to visit
Monsieur Raguideau, a lawyer who had long been
her friend and adviser. Upon arrival at the lawyer's
office, Josephine asked her fiancé to wait in the reception room. She neglected to close the door, however, and he was able to hear their conversation.

When Josephine told her friend of her intention to
marry Bonaparte, he was amazed and did not hide
his disapproval. Napoleon was a mere soldier, an
unknown general without either name or prospects.
"My dear lady," he exclaimed, "think carefully before you take such a step. If you are rash enough to
persist in this preposterous marriage, you will repent
your folly all the days of your life. Who ever heard
of a rational woman throwing herself away upon a

man whose whole fortune consists of his sword and uniform?"

Though listening to this conversation with rising resentment, General Bonaparte determined to say nothing. When Josephine reappeared with Monsieur Raguideau, Napoleon quickly took her arm, and, bowing without a word, withdrew.

A month later, on March 9, 1796, they were married in a civil ceremony. On the marriage contract their ages were both recorded as twenty-eight; Josephine had deducted five years, Napoleon had added one. Two days later he left for Italy to begin his campaign there. Faithfully he wrote daily letters to his beloved wife, fully expressing his adoration. Josephine joined him in Milan to share in his triumphs. She remained in northern Italy for almost two years while he completed the conquest of the rest of the country, winning eighteen major battles and taking 150,000 prisoners. General and Madame Bonaparte were reunited in Paris for only four months, and then Napoleon started his Egyptian campaign.

Josephine enjoyed life while her husband was absent, spending money with extraordinary recklessness. She bought La Malmaison, a palatial château in the country just outside of Paris, and piled up immense debts for its lavish furnishings. When her hus-

band returned in 1799, he paid off her debts in full—
over a million francs.

Hailed as a hero, Napoleon was appointed first
consul of the French Republic. Soon his tenure was
increased to life. Finally, in 1804, the Senate, decid-
ing that France needed "the hereditary rule of a
single man who, raised above all, is to defend public
liberty and maintain equality," proclaimed him emperor.

The coronation ceremony was scheduled for December 2 at the cathedral of Notre Dame. On this
day which marked his attainment of the pinnacle of
power, Napoleon remembered the conversation he
had heard outside the office of Monsieur Raguideau
eight years before. He sent for the lawyer, com-
manding his immediate presence at the Tuileries
palace. The astonished man arrived in breathless
haste and was ushered into a magnificent room
where the first consul and Josephine, dressed in
their coronation robes, were awaiting him.

Napoleon greeted the lawyer with a mischievous
smile. "Ah, Monsieur Raguideau, I am most happy
to see you," he said. "My dear sir," he continued, "do
you remember the day in 1796 when I accompanied
Madame de Beauharnais to your office? Do you remember the unfavorable comments you made on
the military profession and the objections you so

violently expressed concerning her marriage to me?
Well, what do you say now?"

The lawyer stood speechless and trembling, his
eyes on the floor, while the emperor watched him
with amusement, highly enjoying his discomfort. At
last the old man managed to stammer, "Sire, did you
really overhear?"

"Certainly. Every word, Monsieur Raguideau.
And I have not forgotten for these many years since.
You are aware that I should take some revenge upon
you, for if my wonderful Josephine had listened to
your advice, it would have cost her a throne and me
the best of wives."

The old man turned pale. He dared not imagine
what would come next.

The emperor resumed his banter. "I condemn you
to go this day to Notre Dame and to witness my
coronation ceremony in the seat I have reserved for
you. Do you understand, sir? I must see you both
in the cathedral and in the line of the procession."

As they left the cathedral after the coronation,
Napoleon recognized the lawyer in the crowd, and
as their eyes met, the emperor smiled graciously.
The smile was answered by a bow so deep that
Napoleon afterward laughingly declared to Jose-
phine that for several seconds he was in doubt as to

whether Monsieur Raguideau would ever again be able to stand up straight!

The coronation ceremony was one of splendor. Josephine wore a white satin dress with long sleeves, dotted with gold bees and heavily embroidered in gold and silver. Her mantle was of red-orange velvet, with a wide border of ermine. Olive and oak branches were embroidered around the letter N, and it was completely lined with ermine. She literally glittered with pearls and diamonds. The crown consisted of rows of diamonds, emeralds, amethysts, and pearls. Napoleon's breeches were of white velvet, embroidered in gold, with diamond buttons, his short coat was of crimson velvet, his mantle identical with that of his empress, but heavier, weighing more than eighty pounds.

Josephine felt the solemnity as well as the grandeur of the occasion, and later wrote to Pope Pius VII who had come from Rome for the coronation: "Ah, truly do I feel, that in becoming the empress of the French, I ought also to become to them as a *mother* at the same time. What would it avail to bear them in my heart, if I proved my affections for them only by my intentions? *Deeds* are what the people have a right to demand from those who govern them."

As empress, Josephine played her new role with competence. Even though annoyed, she accepted the strict etiquette of the court, and spent many a boring hour receiving and conversing with ministers, marshals, and generals in prescribed ceremonies and receptions. She indulged her chief weakness, extravagance, spending a fortune in clothes and jewels. She always made a favorable impression. Even those who had opposed the monarchy and thought her an upstart of inferior background were forced to admit that she was a worthy consort of the emperor. Her devotion to him was well known and she gained many friends and supporters for him. Napoleon himself said, "I conquer empires, but Josephine wins hearts."

Josephine was forty-one years old when she became empress, but her appearance belied her age. Her features were small and finely modeled. Her eyes were deep blue, her lashes long and silky. Her hair was chestnut brown, her complexion fair. She smiled frequently. Napoleon continued to be bewitched by her and was uninfluenced by his entire family's dislike of her. Whenever he was absent campaigning he wrote to her in detail. She was with him only for the victory celebrations, sharing his military triumphs.

However, one flaw marred their marriage. Josephine had given the emperor no son and heir, and Napoleon dreamed of founding a dynasty. Some say he would have made his stepson Eugene his heir had not the members of his family strenuously objected. The family constantly schemed to turn him against her, even gossiping about her supposed infidelities while he was absent. More and more they pressed him to obtain a divorce. Josephine was quite aware of this intriguing and plotting, which had gone on ever since the coronation. And as the emperor's victories multiplied and his power grew he became completely convinced that he must have a son of his own by a young wife.

The crisis occurred when Napoleon returned from Austria and Germany in the fall of 1809. When he had previously attempted to persuade her that a divorce was necessary, Josephine always objected strongly and warned him against his scheming family and advisers. All of Europe knew that negotiations were under way regarding her successor, who was to be young Marie Louise of Austria, thus linking the house of Hapsburg with France. Josephine, however, was not completely prepared for the shock when it came, for her husband had never ceased to express his continued devotion to her, and she had felt her future was secure.

A letter still exists in which Napoleon told Josephine of his imminent arrival at Fontainebleau after his long absence. He wrote: "I am feasting on the thought of seeing thee again. I embrace thee," and signed it "Ever thine." Those were his words on

October 21, 1809. Yet when he arrived he was cold and formal with her, and she found that he had ordered the door between their bedrooms walled up. Yet he postponed facing the issue and avoided her whenever possible.

Finally, under constant pressure from his political advisers, he could hesitate no longer. The time Josephine had dreaded came after dinner on the evening of November 30, 1809. Napoleon took her hand in his, pressed it to his heart, and spoke the fatal words: "Josephine! My dearest Josephine! You know how I have loved you. To you and to you alone, I owe the only moments of happiness I have had in this world. But my destiny is not controlled by my will. The interests of France must be considered and I must surrender all my personal feelings."

"I understand completely," Josephine replied, tears streaming down her cheeks. "Though I expected this, the blow is not the less severe." And she fainted from shock.

The formal divorce decree was read before the members of the family and court dignitaries on the fifteenth of December. Napoleon spoke first. "God knows what this decision has cost my heart," he said, "but there is no sacrifice which is greater than my courage when it proved necessary to the welfare of France. . . . The memory of the thirteen years of life with my beloved wife will ever be graven in my heart. She has been crowned by my hand. I desire that she keep the rank and title of empress, but before everything else that she never doubt my affection, and that she always regard me as her best and dearest friend."

Josephine, according to custom, had prepared a formal reply, but when the time came for her to speak she was unable to continue after a few sentences, and handed it to the minister of the imperial household for him to finish. She acknowledged that she had no hope whatsoever of bearing more children and that she consented to the dissolution of "a marriage inimical to the welfare of France, whose continuance robs the nation of the happiness of some day being ruled by the descendants of the great man who is its emperor. . . . He will always have in me his best friend. The pain in his heart is shared equally by me."

The settlement was generous. All her debts were paid, and an annual allowance of over half a million dollars granted her. La Malmaison and a palace in Paris were given to her. Josephine sought the seclusion of her beloved La Malmaison. She saw fewer people and spent much time walking through the grounds of her country estate, where she established a beautiful botanical garden, a menagerie, and a school of agriculture.

The marriage contract with the Archduchess

Marie Louise, the eighteen-year-old godchild of the late King Louis XVI and Queen Marie Antoinette, was concluded three months later. In March, 1811, a son was born to the royal couple, named Louis and given the rank and title of king of Rome.

Josephine sent the baby a present of a little carriage drawn by two ponies. Napoleon often made a surprise visit to La Malmaison, talking with his ex-wife as they walked in the famous garden. Josephine was still his most intimate confidante; only to her could he speak freely, sure of never being betrayed and grateful for her good advice.

She was eager to see the son of whom he spoke so proudly. He personally brought the infant to Le Petit Trianon, where Josephine waited. When she looked at the young prince, she said with tears in her eyes, "I am now willing to overlook my husband's treatment of me and concern myself solely with his happiness as a father." This was their last meeting, for he left Paris almost immediately to begin the fatal Russian campaign.

Napoleon's downfall was swift, and the Russians arrived at the very gates of Paris. Marie Louise had long since returned to Austria with their little son. After his exile to the island of Elba, Josephine continued to think of him. She read and reread his letters. One contained the words, "I fear death no longer—to me it would this day be a blessing—but

I would once more see Josephine." She wrote him often, and even offered to share his exile if it were permitted.

Josephine's health had been failing for some time. On the day she died, May 29, 1814, she is said to have looked again and again at a portrait of her ex-husband and exclaimed, *"L'isle d'Elbe—Napoleon!"* The news of her death was heard with sorrow throughout France. Both friends and foes of Napoleon paid tribute to the woman who had brought their emperor such happiness and who was admired for her beauty and intelligence.

And yet, despite Napoleon's careful plans, it was not his son who afterward sat upon the French throne, but, ironically, the grandson of Josephine herself, Napoleon III. He was the son of Hortense de Beauharnais who had married Napoleon's brother Louis and become queen of Holland.

When Napoleon returned to Paris after his final campaign and defeat at Waterloo, he awaited the sentence of his conquerors—exile to St. Helena—at La Malmaison. Time and again he wandered through the empty rooms so full of memories of his beloved empress, saying to himself, "She really loved me, she really loved me."

12

Victoria

1819-1901

The names of few queens have entered the vocabularies of their native languages. In English, Elizabeth is one, Victoria the other. Each of the adjectives, "Elizabethan" and "Victorian," describes an age when England attained its greatest eminence and power, a period when far-reaching changes and reforms were taking place. "Victorian" covers the longest reign of any monarch in English history—sixty-three years—and implies conventionality and scrupulous morality, which were the great queen's outstanding characteristics.

Alexandrina Victoria was born in Kensington Palace in London on May 24, 1819. Her father was Edward, duke of Kent, the fourth son of George III, king of England. Her mother, also named Victoria, was the daughter of the duke of Saxe-Coburg-Gotha. She had been married first to a German prince who left her with two children when he died. After four years of widowhood, she married the duke of Kent. Alexandrina Victoria was their first child.

The parents had chosen the name of Elizabeth for the baby. But at the christening the infant's uncle, the prince regent, substituted the name Alexandrina in honor of her godfather, Emperor Alexander of Russia. Then he added the name Victoria, after her mother. And so, contrary to the wishes of her parents, the child received the name of Alexandrina Victoria.

The following December, while on the coast of Devon with his family for the winter, Edward developed pneumonia. In mid-January of 1820, just before he died, he signed a will making his wife the legal guardian of their daughter.

The duchess of Kent, again a widow, with Victoria not yet a year old, took up residence in Kensington Palace. Her brother, Prince Leopold of Belgium, had offered to increase her inadequate income so that she might remain at the palace with Victoria and her older daughter Feodora. Victoria came to regard Leopold as a father, and was very close to him while he lived in England.

In the family Victoria was called Drina, a shortened form of her first name. She very early began showing signs of willfulness and an uncontrolled temper. To keep the little princess from becoming spoiled, her mother brought Feodora's former governess, Fräulein Louise Lehzen, from Germany. She proved a good teacher, and with tact and firmness won Drina's confidence and love.

The death of the duke of Kent was followed in less than a week by that of King George III, Victoria's grandfather. The prince regent, who had been discharging the royal duties for his sick father, became King George IV.

Drina was seven when she paid her first visit to her uncle, the king. The grossly fat, bewigged monarch was seated in state at the royal lodge, surrounded by his courtiers, when his little niece was presented. "Give me your little paw," commanded His Majesty. Meekly, the child held out her tiny hand, and the king praised her manners and bearing.

Shortly afterward the king saw Drina and her mother in the royal park, stopped his carriage, and said gaily, "Pop her in." The delighted child rode beside her uncle to the river. She was taken aboard a barge from which colorfully dressed lords and ladies were fishing. A band was playing and the king asked his niece what her favorite tune was. Quickly she replied, " 'God Save the King,' sir." The band struck up the national air, and everyone praised the tact of the seven-year-old princess.

Victoria's mother thought it best that she not be told that, as heir to the throne, she would one day be queen. The princess had several tutors, but Fräulein Lehzen still carefully directed her studies and reading. She took music and dancing lessons, and occasionally attended the opera with her mother. She went to bed early and still slept in her mother's bedroom.

The year of Princess Victoria's eleventh birthday, 1830, brought two great changes. King George IV died, and another uncle, William, was crowned king. William IV was far more popular than his brother had been. During his seven years as king he restored to the monarchy a good deal of the prestige it had lost during the previous reign.

The second change ended Victoria's frequent and happy visits with her uncle Leopold in Surrey, for he left England and in 1831 became king of Belgium. Since Victoria had been so close to him, she missed Leopold greatly. But he continued as her friend and adviser, and they wrote long letters to each other for many years.

When sixty-six-year-old William came to the throne, Parliament passed a Regency Bill, stating that if he should die childless, Princess Victoria would be recognized as heir to the throne. If she became queen when still under eighteen, her mother was to be regent. The duchess of Kent was granted an additional annual allowance of ten thousand pounds for "the household and education of Princess Victoria."

When Victoria was twelve, her mother decided that it was time to tell her what the future held. One day Fräulein Lehzen traced the genealogy of English royalty with the princess. As they reached the end, Victoria exclaimed with surprise, "Why, Fräulein, I cannot see who is to come after Uncle William, unless it is myself!" When told that this was true, she said simply, "*I will be good.*"

The years passed by happily. When she was seventeen Victoria's uncle Leopold, always concerned with her welfare, decided that the time had come to select her future husband. Accordingly he sent six of his German nephews, two at a time, to visit her at Kensington Palace. In her diary the princess noted her impressions of each. Cousin Albert of Saxe-Coburg-Gotha proved to be her favorite. He was her own age, fond of music, a gifted pianist, and spoke English fluently, though with a German accent. She liked him, but was not yet interested in marriage.

The coming of age of Princess Victoria was celebrated by a state ball. For her eighteenth birthday present the king gave her a grand piano and a personal allowance of ten thousand pounds a year which made her independent of her mother.

A month later King William, who had been seriously ill, grew suddenly worse. Early in the morning of June 20, 1837, after receiving the last rites of the church, he died, comforted by the knowledge that his niece was no longer a minor and that England therefore would not be ruled by a regent.

The archbishop of Canterbury and the lord chamberlain drove rapidly to Kensington Palace, arriving at five o'clock. Arousing the sleeping servants, they asked to see Victoria at once. She hastily slipped on a dressing gown and entered the sitting room where the two men stood. The archbishop told her what had happened. She was now, he solemnly announced, queen of England.

In one night Victoria's life had changed completely. The first thing she did was to write a letter to her beloved uncle Leopold in Belgium. In her journal she wrote, "I am very young and inexperienced, but I am sure that very few have more real good will and more real desire to do what is fit and right than I have."

At nine that morning the prime minister, Lord Melbourne, arrived in full court dress. The short, fair-haired girl conducted herself with perfect dignity before him. At eleven she held her first council meeting, greatly impressing the assembled dignitaries with her composure and poise. As soon as it was over, she left the room and went straight to her mother.

"Dear Mamma," she said, "I hope you will grant the first request I make to you as queen. Let me be by myself for an hour."

The young queen spent the next sixty minutes alone for the first time in her entire life. The changes to come were baffling to the duchess of Kent, for she had not realized that Victoria, as ruler of England, would be virtually separated from her. First, they moved to Buckingham Palace and Victoria asked for a room of her own, which she had never had before. Then the duchess was assigned a suite of rooms far removed from those of her daughter.

From that time on Victoria assumed all the dignity and prerogatives of a queen. Her mother was allowed no voice in the affairs of state, or in advising her daughter. Victoria appointed Fräulein Lehzen, who had been given the title of baroness, her private secretary and the faithful ex-governess became the new queen's constant companion and confidante.

The coronation was celebrated on June 28, 1838, with the traditional ceremonies. Victoria wore a robe of crimson velvet, trimmed with ermine and gold. Three swords were borne before her—emblems of justice, defense, and mercy. Eight young women of high rank, dressed in cloth of silver with roses in their hair, carried her train.

At the beginning of her reign Victoria was very dependent upon Lord Melbourne, the prime minister. Fortunately, he was devoted to her and counseled her well. She, on her part, was diligent and enthusiastic in carrying out her new duties. As the youthful queen drove about London, she was greeted everywhere with enthusiasm, as a pleasing contrast to her elderly uncles who had ruled England for so long.

By the time she had spent two years in her new role, Victoria had learned a great deal. No longer an inexperienced schoolgirl, she enjoyed both her responsibilities and her newly acquired feeling of independence. She looked forward to the prospect of another visit from her favorite cousin Albert, but was not ready to consider marriage. When he returned to England in 1839, however, Albert had made up his mind that Victoria was to be his wife. He was tired of waiting. As the queen rode horseback, danced, and talked with this attractive suitor, her ideas of marriage suddenly underwent a change. Four days after his arrival, since he could not with propriety propose to her, a sovereign, Victoria asked him to marry her.

The wedding took place on February 10, 1840, at the royal chapel of St. James's Palace. Albert at first found his role as a queen's husband difficult. Lord Melbourne and Baroness Lehzen had much more influence over his wife than he did. Albert was a quiet, reserved man, inclined to be very formal and proper in public, though with friends he was relaxed and warm. In time he and Victoria became closer, and she learned to depend upon him for advice.

Shortly after the birth of their first child, the princess royal, named for her mother, Albert was appointed to act as regent if, in the event of the queen's death, her heir should be under eighteen. In November, 1841, the first son, the prince of Wales, was born. Now Victoria lost her taste for city life and late hours. She was happiest when in the country with Albert and her children. "How blessed I feel in possessing such a perfect being for my husband," she wrote her uncle Leopold.

As the years passed, Victoria continued the wise policies she had adopted during her early years as queen. She followed the actions of her ministers closely, arguing strongly when she did not agree, yet never trying to alter a policy once it had been set by them. Her influence often modified their decisions and she was occasionally successful in averting conflict between the House of Lords and the House of Commons.

Albert became more and more interested in public affairs. He conceived the idea of a great international exposition which would show the progress which had been made in science and industry. He received enthusiastic praise when the immense exhibition building, the Crystal Palace, with its glass roof and elaborate indoor fountain, was at last completed and the exhibition opened in May, 1851. Victoria was delighted with her husband's success. "It was the happiest, proudest day of my life," she reported to her uncle Leopold.

As Victoria and Albert's family increased—eventually there were nine children—the parents felt more and more the need of a retreat from London and Windsor Castle. First they purchased Osborne, an estate on the Isle of Wight. Two years later Albert built a castle, Balmoral, far off in the Scottish Highlands. Here the family enjoyed picnics, walks, and hunting, and Queen Victoria often painted watercolors which were hung on the walls with Albert's hunting trophies. The queen was to spend her happiest days at Balmoral Castle.

But England and Victoria were to experience an unhappy period from 1853 to 1856. The Crimean War, the result of an ill-advised alliance with France against Russia, exacted a heavy price both in the country's young manhood and in money. It was during this war that Florence Nightingale's work as a nurse first attained prominence.

As her daughters passed from childhood, Victoria arranged marriages for them. When the eldest, Vicky, the princess royal, was fourteen, it was settled that she would marry the crown prince of Prussia, Frederick William. The wedding took place in January, 1858, when Vicky was seventeen. Princess Alice was the next to marry, becoming the wife of Prince Louis of Hesse.

Until 1861, when she lost both her mother and her husband, Victoria had known little real sorrow. Early in that year the duchess of Kent died. Then Albert became ill with a fever. He died in December, at the age of forty-two. Toward the end of his life he had become more popular with the people, who had at first considered him an overly serious foreigner. Everyone recognized his enormously valuable influence upon Victoria, who gave him the title of Prince Consort in 1857, and the great contribution he had made to her happiness.

Victoria was overcome with grief, and for years was able to do no more than perform the essential duties of state. To carry on Albert's work was her chief aim. She saw that his speeches were published and in London erected a memorial, Albert Hall, to honor him. Though she withdrew completely from social life and delegated most of the affairs of the kingdom to her prime minister, she continued to be vitally interested in the welfare of her children.

Edward, the prince of Wales, now a young man, had been a source of worry to his parents. He was pleasure-loving, showed little respect for his mother's strait-laced ways, and was completely disinterested in the affairs of the realm. The sudden death of his father, however, brought a sense of responsibility to the prince. Soon after, he fell in love with the Danish princess Alexandra and they were married.

Despite the queen's retirement from public affairs, England continued to prosper. This was almost entirely due to her extremely able prime ministers. These were the days of the great rivalry between William Gladstone, a Liberal, and Benjamin Disraeli, a Conservative, both of whom served Victoria and their country well. The two men were entirely different in their approaches to their sovereign.

Gladstone was always formal and, in deferring to her, he placed the burden of great decisions squarely upon her shoulders. She was never at ease with him, and only after some time did she learn to appreciate his abilities. He was to be her prime minister for fourteen years and the leader of the opposition for an additional twelve years.

Disraeli, on the other hand, was her favorite. He was said to have become as close a friend as it is possible for a queen to have. He was chivalrous, urbane, and shrewd enough to know the psychology of dealing with the queen as both a woman and a ruler. Victoria had complete confidence in him, and the years of his ministry, 1874–1880, were marked by great accomplishments. It was he who was responsible for her gradual emergence from the seclusion she had sought after the death of Albert.

Both of these men aided in the expansion and control of the British Empire. The realm was steadily enlarged until Victoria's dominion finally extended throughout the world—India, Egypt, South Africa and other African possessions, Australia, Canada, and scores of islands, large and small. The saying "the sun never sets on the British Empire" became literally true.

The conquest of the states of India had begun in the previous century, and during Victoria's reign English domination was strengthened, the native princes brought under control, and the country united. The Sepoy Rebellion, 1857–1858, sometimes called the Indian Mutiny, was a black mark on an otherwise successful administration. The prince of Wales was the queen's representative in India in 1875 and 1876, and this was the beginning of his training for his later rule as Edward VII. Through Disraeli's efforts, Victoria acquired the title of empress of India in 1876.

Egypt was added to the British Empire during Gladstone's ministry. The way, however, had been prepared by the far-seeing Disraeli, who in 1875 had gained control of the Suez Canal for England. This was the first step toward British dominance in Egypt, and when England intervened in an internal rebellion in 1882, its armies remained, and the country became a British protectorate.

South Africa proved a trouble spot in the empire. As British colonization spread north from the Cape Colony, the English aided the Dutch Boers in organizing their Orange Free State. But when the Boers were troubled by native uprisings, the British occupied the Transvaal, where the huge diamond mines were located. As more and more British settlers came into the territory the Boers decided that they should be driven out. War was declared in October, 1899, and the struggle was long and bitter, not being ended until 1902, after Queen Victoria's death.

The Victorian age saw the results of the industrial revolution, which had begun in the early years of the nineteenth century. The invention of the steam engine brought a web of railways throughout England and Scotland. The adaptation of steam to sea transport permitted expansion of the empire and commerce with the world. The penny post, with its first adhesive stamp (1841), made internal communication easier, and the electric telegraph (1843) brought the nation and empire closer together.

The greatest change, however, was in the transition from an agricultural to an industrial economy. During Victoria's reign laws designed to improve the status and condition of the workers followed one another in quick succession. There was legislation concerned with trade unions, fair wages, limitation of hours of work, improvement of conditions in factories and mines, and the restriction of child labor. For the first time the workers had a voice in management and began wielding power.

This attention to the individual was reflected also in a vast amount of social legislation—prison reform, housing, schools, and hospitals. One of the great advances was the adoption of universal male suffrage in 1884. Before that time the privilege of voting was based on income or savings; afterward even the poorest man possessed the power of the ballot.

The greatest contribution to the cultural life of the period was in literature. The great English poets, novelists, and essayists of the first half-century— Wordsworth, Byron, Shelley, Keats, Sir Walter Scott, Jane Austen, and Charles Lamb—were replaced in mid-century by other titans. Tennyson, Browning, Swinburne, Dickens, Thackeray, George Eliot, the Brontës, Hardy, Kipling, Stevenson, Carlyle, Ruskin, and Macaulay are but a few in this age of literary productivity. By modern standards most of the painting and sculpture of the Victorian period was mediocre.

Toward the end of the nineteenth century, the population of England had doubled, the country was richer through its expansion of industry and trade, and the British Empire was at the height of its glory.

By then Victoria had become the symbol of the English monarchy, a much-loved queen.

In 1887 England celebrated the fiftieth anniversary of Victoria's reign. Westminster Abbey was crowded for the great event, and royalty from many countries of Europe and representatives from every part of the empire came to pay homage to this remarkable woman. With undiminished energy she continued to fill her days with official duties, letter-writing, and family gatherings. She had long since seen her children and several of her grandchildren married.

In 1897 a diamond jubilee was held in honor of her sixty years as queen. St. Paul's Cathedral was the setting for an impressive religious service. A colorful procession of figures from all over the British Empire escorted Victoria through the streets of London, and a pageant dramatized some of the events of her long reign.

"How kind they are to me! How kind they are!" Her Majesty exclaimed over and over again. Only a few in the vast crowd had ever known any other monarch.

Even in her old age, Victoria was a formidable figure, and both her family and court treated her with great respect. When she died on the twenty-second of January, 1901, after a brief illness, all England mourned the loss of this extraordinary ruler.

Victoria's long reign had spanned nearly the whole of the nineteenth century. She became the symbol of the English monarchy and gave to the throne the permanence which still endures.

13

Tzu Hsi

1835-1908

All queens recognize the power they possess by reason of their exalted position. Some use it for the good of their subjects, others for their own selfish purposes. Tzu Hsi, empress dowager of China, was of the latter type.

Seldom has a monarch possessed such personal and autocratic power and failed to use it for her nation's good. In youth Tzu Hsi was a beautiful concubine. In maturity she was a ruler who held the Chinese Empire and the Manchu dynasty firm against the encroachments of the West during the last half of the nineteenth century.

Although she was descended from one of the oldest Manchu clans, Tzu Hsi was not of royal lineage.

At her birth in November, 1835, her name was recorded in a government book, to which the names of her younger sister and two brothers were later added. All first- and second-rank Manchu officials and their children were so registered.

Little is known of Tzu Hsi's childhood. She used her family name of Yehonala as her given name, and her upbringing probably did not differ much from that of the average upper-class Chinese girl. Living a sheltered life in Peking under the care of her widowed mother, she was never permitted to appear in public and was educated at home. Since she was of high-ranking Manchu ancestry, she was eligible at the age of fourteen to be chosen by the emperor as one of his concubines, called secondary wives. Her training was carried on with this possible end in view.

Yehonala's playmates were Sakota, a distant kinsman, and Jung Lu, a cousin. The paths of these friends crossed many times in later life, and she saw more of them than she did of her own family.

When Yehonala was fifteen years old the emperor Tao Kuang died. At the end of the official twenty-seven-month period of mourning, the new emperor, Hsien Fêng, ordered all Manchu maidens who possessed the proper qualifications for membership in his harem to appear at court.

As daughters of first- and second-class Manchus

of the Bannerman clans, both Yehonala and Sakota were on the list of eligibles, and they passed the preliminary provincial examinations which screened the candidates. The two girls were then taken to the imperial palace where, together with about sixty others, they were inspected by the empress dowager, the widow of the late emperor. As the manager of the royal household, she had full authority to select concubines for her son.

The empress dowager chose twenty-eight, among whom were Yehonala and Sakota. And so it happened that Yehonala remained in the Forbidden City, the part of Peking reserved for royalty. She entered the palace in 1853 as a member of the lowest of the three classes of concubines.

One day, so the story goes, Emperor Hsien Fêng was strolling through the grounds of the palace when he heard a lovely voice singing from behind a shelter of plane trees. He stopped and asked her name, for he had seen but never met Yehonala. Thereafter he was often in her company, even asking her advice on problems of state. More and more it was she with whom he discussed his rule.

After the empress dowager died in 1855, Yehonala was advanced in rank to favorite concubine. Sakota, her childhood friend, was simultaneously made empress consort, a higher rank, but she had no interest in government.

The emperor was overjoyed when in April, 1856, Yehonala gave birth to a son, T'ung Chih, a prince who might become the next emperor of China. She was then raised in rank and called empress mother.

In her new position Yehonala began to wield great influence in court circles. She soon became familiar with the problems of the entire kingdom. When Hsien Fêng was stricken with paralysis he asked her to take over his duties. Her position as mother of the heir apparent and her proven ability to cope with national affairs made her the natural choice.

Slowly and carefully Yehonala built up a group of friends and supporters to whom her very words were law. Among them was Jung Lu, the friend of her childhood, who was an officer in the palace guard. With her increased responsibility and assumption of power came a great change in her disposition. From an amiable young woman always eager to please the emperor, Yehonala became arrogant, willful, and often short-tempered. She was made a Fei, an imperial concubine, the highest rank. Even the emperor himself began to fear her, for he was too sick to oppose her.

A treaty with England and France in 1858 permitted representatives of foreign governments to live in Peking, gave foreigners the right to travel freely throughout the kingdom, and opened the Yangtze River to trade. But these agreements were violated the next year. When negotiations failed, the English and French undertook an invasion of north China, advancing to within two miles of Peking in 1860.

Since he was not prepared to resist, Hsien Fêng ordered the royal household to Jehol, a hundred and fifty miles away, beyond the Great Wall. He appointed his brother, Prince Kung, to negotiate with the foreigners in his name. This was the first time that Yehonala's hatred of foreigners came to the fore. Believing that China should fight to the death against the encroachments of aliens, she opposed this move toward conciliation, but was overruled.

However, she convinced the emperor to let her act for him in relation to Prince Kung and affairs in Peking. From Jehol she directed the defense of the city, even outlining in detail the tactics to be used by the prince. After the summer palace had been burned to the ground by the British, however, Prince Kung surrendered and agreed to peaceful settlement. The terms included payments of indemnities and the release of prisoners, all contrary to Yehonala's directives. In vain she implored the sick emperor to reopen hostilities. Instead, in October, 1861, he confirmed the treaty of peace.

One of the emperor's counselors, Su Shun, was jealous of Yehonala's ever-growing influence. Should Hsien Fêng die, she would become regent during her son's minority. Su Shun therefore joined with two princes in a conspiracy to destroy her future power.

When the emperor's death was near, the three prevailed upon him to sign a decree appointing them as coregents of his successor. The emperor died the next day, and the five-year-old T'ung Chih was proclaimed emperor and the three his guardians.

But the plotters had reckoned without Yehonala. No decree was valid until officially stamped with certain state seals. These seals could not be found at this crucial moment. She had effectively hidden them. Hence the decrees were not yet legal.

The two empresses, Yehonala and Sakota, and the new emperor returned to Peking in advance of the funeral cortege and used the seals to legalize imperial decrees which they issued. They first appointed T'ung Chih ("Universal Tranquillity") as the new emperor of China. He in turn, in spite of his youth, then issued a decree appointing the two women as joint regents during his minority. Sakota, the empress consort, was given the title Tzu An ("Maternal and Peaceful"), and Yehonala, the empress mother, Tzu Hsi ("Maternal and Auspicious"). They were both empress dowagers: Tzu An was to be empress of the eastern palace and Tzu Hsi empress of the western palace.

When the two princes and Su Shun arrived from Jehol with the body of the dead emperor, Tzu Hsi presided at an audience on behalf of her son and ordered their arrest for "high treason and wanton usurpation of authority." After the funeral the two empresses appointed a tribunal to try the three conspirators and they were condemned to death by slow torture. But Empress Tzu Hsi showed clemency. Su Shun was publicly beheaded. Because they were of royal blood, the two princes were given silken cords with which to commit suicide by hanging themselves.

At the age of twenty-six, Tzu Hsi was now more powerful than ever before. Since her associate regent, Empress Dowager Tzu An, continued to take no interest in political affairs, Tzu Hsi was the supreme authority and real ruler of all China. Her overweening greed and lust for authority began to show more and more.

All decrees during this eleven-year regency (1862–1873) were issued under the name of her son, Emperor T'ung Chih. Tzu Hsi was now able to consolidate the position of the Manchu ruling class. A number of rebellions against the central power of the dynasty had broken out and been put down. The empress dowager's second objective, next to her desire to bar foreigners from China, was to strengthen the Manchu hold upon the people.

The two empress dowagers held daily audiences in the palace, with Prince Kung, the emperor's uncle, as their adviser and chief minister, bearing the title prince counselor. Fearing her own inexperience, Tzu Hsi relied upon him for guidance. As she gained confidence she began to resent her minister's independence and to ignore his advice. When Prince Kung dared to question some of her actions she took away his title and for a while banished him from the court.

Tzu Hsi thoroughly enjoyed her exalted position and the power which was hers. She did not, however, use her influence very wisely. She made the mistake of surrounding herself in the palace with eunuchs, whose influence on her was deeply resented.

When T'ung Chih reached the age of seventeen late in 1873, the empress dowagers resigned the regency in his favor, admonishing him to be "thrifty and diligent, endeavoring to make perfect your government." His reign was to be brief.

From the beginning, the spoiled young man was rebellious and disrespectful toward his mother, showing a preference for Tzu An. He refused to consult Tzu Hsi on state business and never asked her advice. After a reign of only a little over two years, T'ung Chih died of smallpox in January, 1875.

With the death of her son, Tzu Hsi no longer ranked as empress mother, and by right of seniority Tzu An should have assumed control. But she was resolved not to yield her place. She called a council meeting immediately. With the aid of her ever-faithful followers, she managed to have her four-year-old nephew declared heir to the throne.

Once more Tzu Hsi had won a complete victory. The two empress dowagers "reluctantly" accepted the coregency again. The new boy-emperor was named Kuang Hsü ("Glorious Succession").

As time went on the little emperor more and more showed a marked preference for Tzu An. Tzu Hsi suspected that Prince Kung, who had been restored to favor, and her coregent were plotting to alienate Kuang Hsü from her. The two empress dowagers quarreled bitterly about precedence. Tzu An, the empress of the eastern palace, attempted to relegate her junior, the empress of the western palace, to second place. More dissension arose over the conduct of the eunuchs and the power they were using.

Shortly after these bitter disagreements, Tzu An was taken suddenly ill with a mysterious malady which proved fatal even before the court physician could be summoned. It was generally believed that some sugar cakes sent to her by Tzu Hsi were poisoned. The truth of the charges has never been verified, nor has Tzu Hsi's innocence ever been proved. The fact remains that those who displeased her failed to survive for long.

For the next eight years Tzu Hsi, as empress dowager, reigned alone, completely dominating the emperor Kuang Hsü. Not until he reached eighteen did she yield the throne to her nephew. She had been regent for fourteen years (1875–1889) and was now fifty-four years old. She retired to the rebuilt summer palace and was inactive for the next ten years, though she continued to hold the emperor in awe of her. She was affectionately referred to as "Old Buddha," from her familiar posture with arms folded over her stomach.

Tzu Hsi had little to do with the disastrous defeat of the Chinese in the Sino-Japanese War of 1894, fought for the possession of Korea. However, the inadequacy of the navy was blamed upon her having diverted funds from naval construction to build a fabulous imperial pleasure garden. The harsh treaty recognized Korea's independence, and Japan was given Formosa.

After the war with Japan the forward-looking emperor Kuang Hsü inaugurated a reform movement to modernize his country. Beginning in 1898, he put into effect improvements in the educational system, developed mines and railways, and reorganized the military and naval forces. Though sympathetic to some of these reforms, the empress dowager felt that these changes were being made too rapidly.

She was alarmed at the "Westernization" of the empire.

The sweeping reforms involved the dismissal and loss of power of many of the entrenched bureaucrats, and were widely denounced by them. A delegation of her former associates visited Tzu Hsi and urged that she resume the throne "to save China from the present disastrous upheaval."

When the emperor was forewarned that his aunt was plotting to thwart his reforms by overthrowing him, he planned to capture Tzu Hsi and confine her on a small island in the lake at the winter palace. But before he could put his scheme into action, the empress dowager arrested him and banished him to a palace on the same island, where he remained for two years.

Tzu Hsi, with the efficiency born of long practice, once more enjoyed her position of power. All her actions were made legal by decrees in Kuang Hsü's name. Her humiliated and heavily guarded nephew retained only the title of emperor.

The Boxer Rebellion broke out in the year 1900. Some of the Chinese were distrustful of the encroachment of the foreigners—English, French, Russians, and Germans—who had obtained valuable trading concessions and ports. A wave of nationalism brought about the formation of many secret societies with the single object of driving the foreigners and everything foreign out of the country. These fanatical nationalists organized into a society called the "Fists of Righteous Harmony," leading foreigners to nickname them the "Boxers."

The foreign powers sent troops to protect their interests and at their approach Tzu Hsi was forced to flee Peking. The summer palace was ransacked, and her throne, the symbol of her power, was cast into the lake. The diplomatic corps in the capital was reduced to a state of siege. When the terms of peace were finally agreed upon, the empress dowager was immensely relieved and, in the autumn of 1901, the court finally returned to Peking.

Not until the Boxer uprising did Tzu Hsi belatedly come to the conclusion that the Chinese Empire must inevitably accept some of the elements of Western civilization which she had so long resisted. In an imperial edict in 1901 she put her seal of approval on the continuance of reforms.

"Any system which has lasted too long," she wrote, "is in danger of becoming stereotyped. Things which are obsolete should be modified. . . . We must strengthen our empire and improve the condition of our subjects. I have now decided that we should correct our shortcomings by adopting the best methods and systems which obtain in foreign countries, basing our future conduct on a wise recognition of past errors." Thus the Old Buddha set in motion a new reform movement. But this was slow in gaining momentum.

The emperor became ill in 1908 and Tzu Hsi, now seventy-three, once more resumed the throne. He died on November 14, and the next day the empress dowager, who had been at his bedside until the end, announced the appointment of Prince Ch'un as regent for his son Pu-yi. Tzu Hsi's niece, the widow of the emperor, became empress dowager, while she became grand empress dowager.

That same day, while at luncheon, the aged ruler collapsed. She regained consciousness, but died that afternoon.

For almost half a century, as regent and coregent, this autocratic woman had controlled the destinies of her people. "A woman with the courage of a man and more than the ordinary man's intelligence," as one historian described her, Tzu Hsi almost single-handedly maintained the power of the Manchu dynasty. Her enemies later charged her with having been responsible for its downfall after a three-century rule of the Chinese Empire.

The empress dowager's weakness was twofold— her love of power and her hatred of foreigners. With dedicated purpose she resisted the Western influences which could have contributed much to the development of China. She could not or would not look into the future.

But with her death the way was open for the long-delayed new order—the rise of the Republic of China.

14

Wilhelmina

1880-1962

To the names of those queens who became symbols to their subjects of the strength of the monarchy, that of Wilhelmina of the Netherlands should be added. Beloved throughout her half-century reign, her absent leadership and encouragement in the dark days of German occupation during World War II reassured her subjects. Her strength became their strength.

In 1880 the sixty-three-year-old king of the Netherlands, William III, and his second wife, Emma of Waldeck-Pyrmont, became the parents of a daughter, the first and only child of their marriage. The girl was christened Wilhelmina after the eight

Williams of Orange in her ancestry. Three, including her own father, had been rulers of Holland and all had made significant contributions to the country's past. They formed an appropriately distinguished background for the child who was to inherit the throne at the age of ten.

Wilhelmina spent her early years in the royal palace at Het Loo in the province of Gelderland. Here she was raised under the watchful eye of her mother, evidently a strong-minded, sensible woman who was the product of an unpretentious country upbringing in Germany. Although Queen Emma had many official duties, she usually found time to play with her daughter or take her riding about the countryside in a wicker carriage drawn by two of her favorite grays or roans. She was a member of the Dutch Reformed Church and she carefully watched over Wilhelmina's religious education. On Sundays the girl listened to her mother tell Bible stories or she memorized Psalms and hymns. This was the beginning of Wilhelmina's interest in religion; it was to grow steadily over the years.

Every day Wilhelmina was allowed to spend an hour with her father. Dressed in her best, she walked eagerly down the great staircase and across the drawing room to his study. Sometimes they played dominoes. Other times they played with the king's new zinc bathtub, a wonderful toy, for one only had to turn on a faucet and the water would come gushing out ready for sailing paper boats.

Outside in the park Wilhelmina had a playhouse, a chalet that was built especially for her. There she drank hot chocolate from tiny cups and helped herself to apricot tarts, gingerbread, nuts, and cookies from plates of the finest china. Nearby were a swing, a seesaw, and a duckpond. She had her own garden and often picked bouquets for her father, who loved flowers. For pets there were rabbits, chickens, and a donkey named Grisette. Later her father presented her with four Shetland ponies which she learned to drive four-in-hand.

At Christmas the family moved from the palace at Het Loo to The Hague, where they remained until after Easter. Then they paid a visit to Amsterdam. Sometimes they also visited the queen's parents at Arolsen. Usually they traveled by trains, which were very comfortable in those days.

When Wilhelmina was seven, her father became ill. For the next three years this illness placed a great strain upon the household which she noticed and worried about. When he felt well enough, she was able to see him, and he tried to think up things that would please her. He added a kitchen to the chalet, so Wilhelmina could cook there.

When William III died in 1890, Wilhelmina was frightened by the visitors, dressed in black, who came to extend their condolences. She had to stand beside her mother and receive them. The funeral, too, was very upsetting, and afterward she was put to bed with a stomachache. Although she knew she had succeeded to the throne she did not understand how she would ever be ready to take on the burdens which would come with her coronation at the age of eighteen. Meanwhile, her mother was made regent, and she tried to explain to Wilhelmina the meaning of her future. Wilhelmina wrote of this period in her autobiography, *Lonely But Not Alone:* "I pulled myself together and put my problems before Mother. We had a long and deeply serious talk about them. I was struck with awe at the thought that only eight years would have to suffice for me to become grown up and wise and sensible, and I saw that there was no time to be lost. I resolved and promised Mother to work as hard as I could, unremittingly."

Wilhelmina's education was supervised by her mother and a series of governesses and tutors. She studied arithmetic, art, geography, literature, Dutch history, and languages. There were also piano lessons, but Wilhelmina had no ear for music and was glad when they stopped. She did not like her dancing lessons either and was always stubborn about learning something that did not interest her. She did enjoy drawing and painting and often took her sketchbooks with her out of doors and drew horses and dogs. Although her father had forbidden her to learn to skate, since it was considered improper for girls, she did so secretly. She also played tennis and rode horseback. With her mother she traveled about Holland and Europe. The tutors usually went along, too, so her studies would not be interrupted. She visited England, where she met Queen Victoria, and Weimar, Germany, where at a family reunion she was introduced to a sixteen-year-old boy who was destined to become her husband. His name was Hendrik of Mecklenburg.

Gradually Wilhelmina was exposed to the responsibilities of government and she attended the opening of the States General in Amsterdam. With so many demands on her time, there were few moments to be alone or to relax. "I could only be an ordinary human being when I was alone with Mother," she wrote in her book. "The palaces themselves bore the mark of formality, one had to look hard for a corner that was comfortable and simply human." She was seldom able to play with children her own age. When they did visit, they came in groups and played in a large formal drawing room. She felt as though she were in a cage and frequently longed for freedom.

Wilhelmina came of age on August 31, 1898. At the exact moment she turned eighteen she put her signature to some official documents, and so signified the beginning of her reign. She was installed as queen of the Netherlands in an impressive, formal ceremony in the Nieuwe Kerk in Amsterdam. Later she described her feelings on this awesome occasion: "At last the moment arrived when I had to leave my rooms. The train of the royal mantle was taken up by the bearers. All the standards of the army, which were to precede me, were lowered. Overwhelming experience for me, who received this salute for the first time.

"Then all took up their places and we walked slowly past the ranks of servants, so many faithful old faces, betraying their emotion. It seemed an eternity in that deathly silence and in my mood of loneliness and desolation.

"Then we had to descend the high staircase. Would I still be able to utter a word in church? Would I still have a voice? In that silence in which one could have heard a pin drop, I addressed the nearest trainbearer: 'All right so far, Mr. Grovestins?' What a relief, my voice was still there! 'Excellent,' came the answer."

When the service was over, everyone in the church joined in the joyous cries of *Leve de Koningin,* "Long live the queen!"

After six weeks of receptions and meetings, the new queen returned to Het Loo, where life seemed to go on as before, quiet and confining, always according to the well-established routine. "Little or nothing ever happened," said Wilhelmina. "Even if I had tried, I would have changed nothing."

In the summer of 1900 she and her mother visited a mountain resort in Germany, which was the family seat of the Schwarzburgs, the grandparents of Hendrik. Hendrik was there, too, for a holiday and to pay a call on Wilhelmina. She missed him after he left, for she had fallen in love, and once back in Holland she waited anxiously for a letter. Finally he wrote, asking to see her again, and they met at the home of another relative in Germany. Hendrik had to travel incognito to avoid being questioned by newspaper reporters who suspected a romance. He and Wilhelmina made their decision quite suddenly one day, just after they had been left alone following a family luncheon.

"Ten minutes later," Wilhelmina recorded, "we returned and announced our engagement. The die was cast. What a relief that always is on these occasions!"

The wedding took place on February 7, 1901, in Holland. There was great rejoicing on the part of the families and of the Dutch people. The young couple received many lavish gifts, including a golden coach which the city of Amsterdam presented to the queen.

Hendrik, who had been raised in the country,

was an enthusiastic outdoorsman. His main interests were the fine horses he bred, hunting, and forestry. He spent much time in the woods and working on reforestation and conservation projects. Wilhelmina described him as having "a kind and open nature" and "always willing to help." She went on, "Simplicity was his first characteristic. He was simple in his manner, in his tastes, in his character."

Once married, Wilhelmina felt a strong desire to break away from her dependence on her mother and establish her own life with Hendrik. Convention and public opinion restricted her, but she struggled against both. When she and Hendrik did anything out of the ordinary, they were criticized. Most of the time, however, their lives were uneventful. There were parties with friends, visits about Europe, and tours of Holland when Wilhelmina gave speeches, which she insisted on writing herself.

In 1909, after waiting eight years for a child, Wilhelmina and Hendrik were overjoyed at the birth of a daughter. They named her Juliana. When she was five they took her to The Hague where they stayed at Huis ten Bosch, a royal residence which had been vacant since 1877.

"The house was furnished in the worst possible taste," wrote Wilhelmina, "and signs of decay were everywhere. We considered ourselves lucky if we could find one oil-lamp for each room. The walls

of these rooms one should imagine padded with a
dusty woollen material. . . . The colours were
dark, red or blue. It was too frightful for words."

They redecorated the house, however, and Wilhelmina grew to love it. She lived there during
World War I when she guided her country through
an uneasy period of neutrality. During this time the
problems of leadership were many, but Wilhelmina
admitted that she developed greater self-confidence
as a result of having to cope with them. The war
also gave her an opportunity to cut down the size of
her staff, for many of the men on it joined the army.
She was glad to simplify her household procedures
and considered this one more victory in her struggle
to break out of what she called her "cage."

When she inspected troops or took part in any
sort of official tour, she always made an effort to
talk directly with the people. Expressing her wish to
broaden her experience, she said, "I wanted to meet
people as they really were, not dressed up for a visit
at the palace." Some of her associates understood this
desire and supported it. Others did not.

In the unrest that followed the war certain Dutchmen stirred up feeling against the monarchy and its
conservative traditions. In protest, thousands of
demonstrators expressed their loyalty to the crown
at a mass meeting in The Hague, to which the queen,
Hendrik, and Juliana were invited. Spontaneously,

the crowd unhitched the horses which were harnessed to the royal carriage and drew Wilhelmina triumphantly across the square. Later there was a similar demonstration in Amsterdam, and many other expressions of support.

Holland's joining of the League of Nations forced many citizens, including the queen, into a greater awareness of world affairs. There were serious unemployment problems, too, upon which she had to act. Advisory boards kept her informed and counseled her on these matters.

Wilhelmina began to devote some of her time to the study of art. She took lessons from accomplished teachers and liked to draw conventional landscapes. When she traveled to Norway with Hendrik in 1921 to hike and mountain climb, she took her paints and brushes with her. In the spectacular mountain scenery she felt very close to God and found the strength to return to her tasks. "Art is a part of religion to me," she said.

In 1934 Wilhelmina's mother, Emma, died and was buried beside her husband, King William, in the Nieuwe Kerk in Delft. While the queen was recovering from this tragedy in Switzerland, word came that Hendrik had suffered a serious heart attack. She hurried home to find him failing, and a few days later he died. Because neither Wilhelmina nor Hendrik thought of death as an end, but rather as a beginning, they had agreed to have white funerals. To them white symbolized eternal life. This unusual arrangement was now observed and made a startling impression upon the people of the country. After the funeral the distraught queen and her daughter went to Norway for solitude and rest.

In contrast, Juliana's wedding in 1937 to Prince Bernhard of Lippe-Biesterfeld was an occasion for much rejoicing. A year later Wilhelmina became grandmother to a girl, Beatrix, and the following year a second grandchild, Irene, was born.

When World War II broke out in Europe, Holland once again issued a statement of neutrality. However, it was not respected by the German armies who crossed the Dutch frontier just as German paratroopers were dropping over The Hague. Wilhelmina and her family, shocked by the fearful turn of events, remained close to their air raid shelter in the garden, while confusion reigned in The Hague and throughout the country. Bernhard devised a plan for transporting Juliana and the children to England. Wilhelmina insisted he accompany them and was enormously relieved when word came that they had reached their destination safely.

Wilhelmina herself believed she could remain at her post in The Hague, but within a few days she realized that her small army was no match for the Germans. Though her commander-in-chief advised her to try to reach England, she was filled with conflicting emotions, for she was well aware of the impression her departure would make at this terrible moment of invasion. Yet she also knew that for the best interests of the Netherlands, the seat of government had to be preserved. She decided to go to Zeeland, Flanders, a part of the country still believed to be safe. At the Hook of Holland she boarded the British destroyer that was to take her there. Once on board, however, the queen found that the ship's commander was forbidden to make contact with the shore.

"This was very disappointing news," the queen wrote, "for it practically meant the end of our plan to go to Zeeland. It would have been completely irresponsible to arrive there without previously notifying the rear-admiral, who would have been responsible for the conduct of the war as well as my personal security; and we knew nothing of the military situation in Zeeland. What could we do? By this time we were in open sea, there could be no question of going back. After consultation with those whose opinion should be heard—a miniature war council in life-jackets—I decided to go to England."

Once in England she was welcomed by Juliana and by King George who took her to Buckingham Palace. She then issued a proclamation to her people, explaining why it was necessary to transfer the seat of government and so avoid being forced to surrender to the enemy. She made a plea for courage on the part of those who remained in occupied territory.

In June of 1940 Juliana and her children were sent to Canada for the duration of the war. The queen moved to a small cottage outside of London, which served as a rallying point for Dutchmen in England. She was kept informed on the progress of the war, although for a long time it was difficult to get accurate news of what was happening in Holland. Her life was dominated not "by action," she reported, "but by endless waiting; by the expectation of the day when the people of the Netherlands, delivered from the power of the enemy, would resume control of their own destiny." She tried to encourage her subjects in her speeches to them over the radio, assuring them that the Netherlands would be liberated. During this difficult time, Wilhelmina was helped by her deep religious beliefs. She spent many nights in air raid shelters, carrying her important papers with her.

A center for the Free Dutch was established in London. Dutchmen who had escaped from Holland, as well as Dutch from all parts of the world, gathered here. On the day the center was dedicated Queen Wilhelmina wore a marguerite, the white flower so common at home, which she had chosen as a symbol of the hope that Holland would soon be free.

In 1942 the queen flew in an airplane for the first time. The plane had been sent to England by President Franklin D. Roosevelt to bring her to the United States. First there was a happy reunion in Ottawa with Juliana and the children. Then she visited Hyde Park, New York, where she met President Roosevelt, who impressed her with "his strong personality, his will-power and his perseverance." She noted, too, that Mrs. Roosevelt was "a very independent woman." She addressed the United States Congress, and saw Mount Vernon, Albany, New York City, and Boston. After returning to Ottawa, she bid her daughter and grandchildren good-bye and flew back to England.

Finally in 1945 the retreat of the Germans and the liberation of three provinces in Holland made it possible for Wilhelmina to set foot once again on her native soil, even though the war was not yet over. She went first to Belgium and then set out by automobile for the Dutch frontier. When she reached it, she got out of her car and crossed on foot. A tumultuous welcome awaited her. "Wherever I went, the same emotion and enthusiasm," she described it later. "Everywhere flowers, presents and all sorts of attention. In every town and village resistance workers and widows and children of fallen underground fighters were presented to me at my special request."

The queen had to go back to England, but finally the day came when she and Juliana could return to Holland for good. "What an unforgettable journey it was! Our exile had come to an end, Juliana and I returned home."

The war had left great devastation in Holland. Dams had been bombed and farm lands were flooded. Villages, factories, canals, and roads had been destroyed. Holland's allies began to drop food from the air to help prevent widespread starvation, for there was nothing to eat. A new cabinet had to be formed, so it could begin the task of governing, of building order out of chaos, and the queen chose as her advisers men who had been active in the resistance to the German occupation. Millions of dollars worth of aid came to Holland from the Marshall Plan of the United States. Slowly production was resumed and agriculture began to flourish once again, and in the months and years that followed, Holland gradually worked its way back to prosperity, though the queen would never forget the horror and suffering of her people during the war.

As the years passed, Wilhelmina began to think of retiring. She designated Juliana as regent, so her daughter would have an opportunity to learn about the responsibilities which lay ahead for her, and then planned her abdication. Her sixty-eighth birthday was approaching. It coincided with the fiftieth anniversary of her reign and a large jubilee celebration was being organized. The queen did not feel equal to so much festivity and wanted to retire quietly before her birthday, but she was persuaded not to. However, she did insist on announcing that her abdication would take place immediately afterward.

On the fourth of September, 1948, Queen Wilhelmina's reign of half a century came to an end. The act of abdication was read aloud and she signed it. "The ceremony had been a short one," she wrote, "there was a long time to wait before noon would be announced by the chimes of the palace clock, followed by its twelve powerful strokes. . . . When the twelfth stroke had sounded the balcony doors were opened and . . . I . . . introduced Juliana to the people of the Netherlands as their Queen." It was a very emotional moment and when the festivities were over and Wilhelmina was alone she felt great relief that it was behind her.

The retired queen was able to go on living at Het Loo, though she moved to another wing of the palace. At first she felt tired and lonely. She gave up her committee work, not only because she did not want to interfere with Juliana but also because she wished to be free to spend her time painting, writing, or with her grandchildren. There were now four girls and they gave her great pleasure. She requested permission to use her childhood name, Princess Wilhelmina, once again, and it was granted.

In her old age Wilhelmina thought more and more about her religious beliefs. It was difficult for her to find inner peace, for without her role as queen she felt purposeless. However, she came to the conclusion that she had "become a world citizen in the spiritual sense," that she was "touched by that love of all mankind which springs from Christ Himself," and that this had been her true purpose throughout her life.

She died peacefully in her sleep on November 28, 1962, at the age of eighty-two.

15

Juliana

1909-

On April 30, 1909, a rousing salute of fifty-one guns rang out in the early morning, proclaiming to the people of the Netherlands the birth of a princess, the daughter of Queen Wilhelmina and Prince Hendrik. The new heir to the throne, born in the royal palace at The Hague, was christened Juliana Louise Emma Marie Wilhelmina, a long name for a small baby, but it was the custom of Dutch nobility to so honor its ancestors. The Juliana was after Juliana van Stolberg, the mother of William of Orange who had founded the Dutch nation. Louise was for William's fourth wife; Emma for Queen Wilhelmina's mother; Marie for Hendrik's mother, the grand duchess of Mecklenburg; and last,

Wilhelmina was for the queen herself. The Dutch people, however, called the little princess "Julia-antje."

Wilhelmina received many expressions of good will at the birth, but one always stood out in her mind. It was a letter describing the contribution Juliana van Stolberg had made to Holland and a light blue belt which had been embroidered with oranges, the family symbol.

Juliana grew up at Het Loo, the country palace where her mother had been raised before her. The queen was determined that her daughter should have more freedom than she had experienced in her childhood, for she did not want her to feel the restrictions and loneliness that had always surrounded the royal household. So she made an effort to spend as much time as she could with Juliana, particularly in autumn and summer, when she put aside all but the most pressing official duties, and she encouraged the visits of other children. Juliana played in the chalet which had been built for Wilhelmina, though now there was a balcony and the walls were painted with bright designs.

In 1913, when Juliana was four, her family spent some time in a house in Apeldoorn, while Het Loo was being renovated, and it was a treat to be in a normal-sized home. One day there was a party for Juliana and the staff children with a circus performance on the lawn in front of the stables. Then the children played games, including one called "Such Are Our Manners," where Juliana stood in the center of a circle and with poise demonstrated the fine points of etiquette to the group.

When World War I began, Juliana was only five and did not really understand what was happening. She remembered it mainly as a time at Huis ten Bosch, a palace in The Hague that was located on an island surrounded by moats. This meant rides in a rowboat for the princess, who sometimes dipped her net into the water to catch frogs. She had a pet fawn, which she raised on a bottle, as well as horses and dogs. She liked to name the horses on the family estates and often took the names from children's books she had read. Her mother once purchased a black horse which Juliana called Black Jacob after a story about a crow. Jacob was scrawny as a crow when he arrived, for he had been used on the battlefield and was half starved. Later, after careful feeding, he improved and was used in parades where he behaved perfectly unless he heard gunfire. Then no one could prevent him from bolting.

Juliana learned to ride on an Irish bay called Zedda and she liked to show off the tricks she could do. Her mother once wrote that Juliana "asked for two other horses to be put side to side with Zedda and then she climbed across their backs, shouting for joy all the while. She was so cheerful and her little voice was so noisy that she sometimes set the whole cavalcade moving and we really had to teach her to be a little quieter with the horses."

Wilhelmina, who had always been self-conscious about showing her feelings and fearful of appearing too fond of animals lest she be laughed at, wanted her daughter to be able to enjoy her pets openly. Juliana was also free to learn to ice skate, swim, and sail. She rode her bicycle about the country and in the city, too, much to the astonishment of the populace, who had never seen royalty behave so naturally.

A well-known Dutch educator, Jan Ligthart, was responsible for Juliana's first schooling. The queen, who had studied his methods and visited his school, invited him to the palace to observe Juliana so he could recommend the best possible approach to her education. Then a class was formed at Huis ten Bosch and conducted by one of Mr. Ligthart's teachers.

After the age of ten, Juliana was privately tutored. Her primary school teacher stayed on to make the transition less difficult, and a governess who taught French joined the staff. Since it was known that at eighteen Juliana might have to assume the throne, in the event of her mother's illness or death, her education was speeded up. She studied Latin and Greek,

German, English, history, geography, and mathematics.

Her mother was determined that Juliana would not be forced into piano lessons, as many children were, so she permitted her to choose the instrument she wanted to study. Juliana picked the violin and played it for several years. She had a good ear for music and liked to sing, so a singing group was begun for her. She was taught drawing, too, by a teacher who encouraged her to develop her own designs and techniques and who later taught her art history as well.

Juliana begged to have children come to play with her, and her mother frequently invited them to the palace. When the princess was older she went to summer camp. There she met girls from backgrounds which differed from her own and often brought them home for weekends. These friends introduced her to other young people and she developed a large group of acquaintances.

Juliana traveled throughout Europe with her parents, for they felt it was important that she become familiar with other countries and other peoples. She was allowed to spend some of her vacations in Switzerland, Norway, and England, and, of course, she came to know her own country well.

In 1927 Juliana celebrated her eighteenth birthday and officially came of age, according to the

Dutch constitution. There were toasts and speeches in her honor at a small dinner party given by her parents. Afterward the party went into town to see the Parliament buildings, which had been beautifully illuminated for the occasion, and to cruise about a lake in boats hung with brightly glowing lanterns.

Although Juliana was now of age and received her own income, she was still very much under the eye of her mother. Her first official public appearance was in a small town that had been hit by a cyclone. Her mother took her there to talk with victims of the disaster and to observe what had happened. At the same time she was assigned her first political position as a member of the state council, the queen's highest advisory body. Each year from then on, on the third Tuesday in September, she enjoyed the privilege of riding in the famous golden coach that carried the queen to the opening of the States General.

In June, 1927, Juliana was confirmed in the Dutch Reformed Church, sharing the service with a number of other people. She insisted that the ceremony be simple, and no relatives or friends were invited. The minister who had supervised her religious education was there to welcome her into the congregation.

For some years Juliana had been hoping she could attend Leyden University, the oldest and most famous university in Holland. Since there was no precedent for such a decision, and also because Queen Wilhelmina regarded intellectualism with suspicion, there was some doubt as to just what to do. However, Juliana wanted very much to have the opportunity to live and study exactly like any other student, so it was decided that she could matriculate. In autumn of 1927 she and three friends moved to a house near Leyden. The girls, who had a chaperone living with them, called themselves "The Merry Sea Stars" and embraced university life with great enthusiasm.

Juliana's lecture schedule had been arranged by the rector of the university. Since she had not taken the usual preliminary examinations, she could not qualify for the university examinations. Without these exams, she seemed to lack incentive, so a detailed plan of study was drawn up for her. She was required to take a course in international law, and she chose two other courses—comparative religion and modern Dutch literature. She spent her last college year preparing herself for examinations in these three subjects. At the close of the year, she took the exams and an honorary degree of doctor of literature and philosophy was conferred upon her. Then, as was traditional, the completion of her university studies was celebrated by a dinner party at home. Afterward she was taken to Germany for a skiing holiday and then to Norway and Denmark.

During the years at Leyden Juliana made many friends and often brought them to Het Loo for houseparties. She belonged to a club, called *De Zestigpoot,* and its members, as well as "The Merry Sea Stars," came for visits. Sometimes they played the piano and sang student songs until late at night. It was not considered proper for the queen and her husband to join the parties. However, Queen Wilhelmina's exposure to university life through her daughter helped her to overcome some of her prejudices against the intellectualism which she had felt was incompatible with religious belief.

When the world-wide economic depression of the 1930's spread to Holland, many people lost their jobs, and Juliana, who had been doing what would now be called social work in the town of Apeldoorn, was disturbed. She rallied sixty leading citizens around her and formed a "National Crisis Committee." Its purpose was to cope with some of the social problems caused by the depression. During the next five years she devoted much time and energy to this work.

In June, 1934, when Juliana was in England at Kensington Palace visiting a cousin of her mother's, she received word that her father had suffered a heart attack. Before she could return home, her mother phoned to say he had died. Juliana left London immediately by boat and was met at the dock by her mother early the next morning. It was a sad time for the only child of the royal couple; on her shoulders fell most of the burden of supporting the queen during this dark period.

After her father's death, Juliana took over his duties as head of the Dutch Red Cross. In the spring of 1935 she attended the World's Fair in Brussels and was a guest of King Leopold and his wife, Astrid. That summer there was a pleasure trip to Scotland and the next winter another trip took her to the Olympic Games in Bavaria. There she met a young German prince, Bernhard of Lippe-Biesterfeld, who spent several days skiing with her. Bernhard was the scion of a noble but impoverished family. He was planning a career in business and at that time was working for I. G. Farben, the German chemical company.

Juliana was twenty-seven and for some years there had been much speculation about a possible husband for the only heir to the Dutch throne. Names of eligible bachelors cropped up in the newspaper reports of her social activities, but she kept her own feelings on the matter to herself. Juliana has been described as an "unromantic princess." Like her mother she was rather plain, with a round face and strong features which seemed to reflect her solid Dutch character. She was plump and wore her long blonde hair parted in the middle and wound in a braid around her head.

Bernhard, however, seemed attracted by the shy, plain princess who was two years older than he. He went several times to Holland to see her. Friends helped keep his visits a secret, hoping to avoid the publicity that accompanies any royal romance. Later he and Juliana, who was always chaperoned by her mother, met in Weissenburg, Switzerland, and there they became engaged. They wanted to keep the engagement a secret for a while, but public interest brought on all kinds of rumors, and they were soon forced to announce it. Because Bernhard was German and the German regime of the Nazi Adolf Hitler was extremely unpopular in Holland, careful investigation of his political ideas was necessary before the queen and the Netherlands government would give approval to the match.

The young couple was married in 1937 on January 7, the wedding date of Juliana's grandparents, King William and Emma of Waldeck-Pyrmont. After the driving rain of the day before, which had soaked the orange and white streamers decorating The Hague, the clear blue sky was a welcome sight. To the cheers of the thousands of well-wishers who lined her route, Juliana rode in the golden coach to the Church of St. James. She wore an ivory satin gown and a veil embroidered with silver and crowned with orange blossoms. Two boys and two girls, chosen from the children of The Hague, carried her long train. Bernhard was dressed in the handsome captain's uniform of the Blue Hussars, a crack cavalry regiment to which he had been appointed. There were twelve bridesmaids, some university friends from middle-class families, others from the nobility, and twelve ushers. According to law, Bernhard at once assumed the nationality of his wife and became a Dutch citizen.

Juliana set aside fifteen specially printed copies of the wedding program to be sold later at 1000 guilders apiece. To each program was attached a tiny sample of her wedding gown. The proceeds from this unusual sale went to the Dutch Winter Relief Fund, of which Juliana was president.

To confuse the reporters, Juliana and Bernhard left their wedding breakfast by car as was expected, but went only as far as the stables. They reappeared some time later at their reception, much to the astonishment of the guests who greeted them with cheers. They stayed and danced until the party ended, when their friends formed a circle around them and sang "Lang zullen se leven," a popular Dutch toast. The next morning they took the train for Poland and a ski resort in the Carpathian Mountains.

Unfortunately, the wedding festivities were not

without their unpleasant moments, a result of the strong anti-German sentiment in Holland. Juliana was criticized for marrying a German, and Bernhard was sharply reproved by the German newspapers for not doing something about the anti-Nazi feeling in Holland. They called him a "man without character and unworthy of respect" in an emotional piece of party propaganda denouncing any German who did not continue to support Germany. The German secret police confiscated the passports of three of the bridesmaids, German friends of Bernhard's, and he had to write to Adolf Hitler himself to have the passports restored to their owners. Even so, one bridesmaid was "prevented from attending."

After a four-month honeymoon Juliana and Bernhard, now the prince consort, returned to The Hague and moved into the palace of Soestdijk, an attractive, white, rambling country place which was to be their home. Already it seemed as though Juliana had blossomed, for she had developed an interest in clothes and took the advice of a beauty specialist who saw that she lost considerable weight and learned how to use makeup properly. There were complaints about Juliana's traveling on Sundays during her honeymoon, as well as about her plucked eyebrows, but generally people seemed to feel that a bit more spirit in the stodgy Dutch court was a good thing. She modernized Soestdijk, which had not been changed for fifty years, installing central heating, tennis courts, and a swimming pool.

Six months after they had been home and were looking forward to the birth of their first child, Bernhard was seriously injured in an automobile accident. His car collided with a truck which turned unexpectedly onto the road in front of him. Juliana left Soestdijk as soon as she heard the news and, with her mother, hastened to the Amsterdam hospital where Bernhard had been taken. She stayed there for over a month, anxiously watching her husband's progress. Their first Christmas together was spent here, though they appeared to take their bad luck in good spirits. Their Christmas card showed a picture of a wrecked car and under it a humorous verse about the scene being "a lesson to all." Bernhard was released in time for the birth of his first child on January 31, 1938. They named the infant girl Beatrix. A second girl, Irene, was born a year and a half later.

World War II brought an abrupt end to Holland's traditional neutrality, when the German armies invaded the country. Juliana and her two daughters were hurriedly escorted from The Hague to the coast where a British destroyer took them to England. Bernhard went with them to London and then returned to be with Queen Wilhelmina. Finally, he, too, had to flee when the queen decided that the government would have to be carried on in exile. In London the king of England appointed him liaison officer between the British army headquarters and the Dutch armed forces. Because he was particularly interested in the air force, he requested and was given pilot training. His role was difficult, for feeling against all Germans ran high. He was cut off from his family in Germany and, soon, from his wife and children as well.

Juliana's safety seemed paramount, for she was the future ruler of Holland. As the war came closer and closer to England, it was decided that she should go to Canada. Before leaving, the baby, Irene, was christened in the Buckingham Palace chapel. Then Juliana and the children boarded a ship for Halifax, their departure a closely guarded secret. Bernhard saw them off and returned, disconsolate, to London.

Juliana made her headquarters in Ottawa, where the Canadian government installed her in a comfortable house in suburban Rockcliffe Park. There she devoted her time to her family, entertained visiting Dutchmen, and directed the Netherlands Red Cross in exile. She visited President Franklin D. Roosevelt in the United States on good-will missions and flew to the Dutch colonies of Surinam and the Netherlands West Indies. A third daughter, Margriet, was born in 1943, and Bernhard came to Ottawa for the occasion. The hospital room was declared extra-territorial soil by the Canadian government, so that Margriet would be born Dutch rather than Canadian. She was named for the marguerite, the flower that symbolized the Dutch hope for a liberated Holland.

Juliana returned home before the war was officially over, when some of the Dutch provinces had been freed by advancing Allied armies. In 1947, settled once again in beloved Soestdijk with her family, she gave birth to a fourth daughter, Maria Christina. The same year she was designated regent and in 1948, upon abdication of her mother, she became queen at the age of thirty-nine.

In the square before the palace in Amsterdam, thousands of people waited to greet their new queen after the formal act of Wilhelmina's abdication. On the stroke of twelve, Juliana, accompanied by her mother and her husband, appeared on the balcony. Not a whisper could be heard as Wilhelmina began to speak. "I consider it an honor," she announced in a loud, clear voice, "to be able to tell you myself I have just signed an abdication on behalf of my daughter."

Juliana stepped forward, but her eyes were full of tears and she was unable to say a word. Her prepared speech fluttered to the floor and the old queen leaned over to retrieve it. A great shout went up and the crowd began to sing the Dutch national anthem,

"The Wilhemus," followed by an ancient folksong called "We Will Never Give Up Holland." By this time Juliana had recovered herself and was able to say a few words which expressed her gratitude to her mother and her hopes for the future. The four girls, dressed in red dresses and white hair ribbons, came out. Beatrix, age ten, the next in line for the throne, appeared to enjoy the public appearance the most.

After becoming queen, Juliana continued to live at Soestdijk, for she seemed to prefer its informality. She gradually did away with much of the ceremony in the court, though there were some who argued it was necessary to the monarchy. Juliana, however, insisted that it was not and that she was entitled to a normal family life. She planned the meals, played with the children, and guided their education. She wanted to give them more freedom than she had experienced and once said that each generation has to rebel against the one before. Her children attended progressive schools with commoners and the queen discussed mutual problems with other parents.

In 1952 the queen and her husband paid their first official visit to the United States. In the following years they traveled on many good-will tours. Sometimes the trips were by private plane with Bernhard at the controls. Visiting royalty and other distinguished guests, including Mrs. Franklin D. Roose-

velt, often stayed at Soestdijk. Despite Juliana's
many public appearances, she is ill at ease socially
and seems to lack self-confidence. She appears more
relaxed when Bernhard is with her, for he is open
and friendly and finds it easy to make conversation.
However, she has a good mind and her intelligent
questions are respected by her ministers. She writes
her own speeches, which are forthright and sometimes moving, a surprising contrast to her usual dif-
fident manner.

In 1962 the joint celebration of Juliana's fifty-third
birthday and twenty-fifth wedding anniversary gave
the Dutch people an opportunity to demonstrate
their affection for their sovereign and her family.
Juliana's wedding anniversary was actually January
7, but she postponed its observance until spring. On
the festival day the sun shone and a brisk wind
whipped the red, white, and blue flags and orange
streamers which decorated the streets of Amsterdam.
Thousands of loyal subjects waved and cheered as
Juliana and Bernhard toured the city in a cream-
colored coach, followed by the four princesses who
rode in their own red coach. Later the party boarded
a barge and were rowed by twenty midshipmen
along the Amstel River, while people crowded the
banks to watch and applaud. That night the streets
were jammed with noisy celebrants in costumes of
all kinds, caught up in the gay, carnival spirit. The

two days of festivities closed with a ball for visiting royalty on board the liner *Oranje*, as it sailed along the North Sea Canal.

Clearly prosperous, democratic Holland still cherishes the traditional pomp and splendor that sometimes marks the life of its royal family. Yet the people also approve of their queen's simple ways and her efforts to live like any other Dutch wife and mother. The difficult transition from the formal manners of earlier times to a more flexible monarchy attuned to the problems of the twentieth century has been made with considerable grace by Holland's unpretentious queen.

16

Elizabeth II

1926-

On May 29, 1926, a simple but important christening took place in the private chapel at Buckingham Palace. The archbishop of York baptized the month-old daughter of the duke and duchess of York with water from the River Jordan and gave her the name of Elizabeth Alexandra Mary. The small group of guests included the baby's parents and her four grandparents, King George V of England and Queen Mary, and the earl and countess of Strathmore. Elizabeth's christening robe of ivory lace had been worn by four earlier rulers of England, including Queen Victoria. So the tradition that had evolved about the world's most brilliant and respected monarchy began to cast its shadow on the girl who would never be allowed the comfortable anonymity that every other Englishman had the right to enjoy.

The duke and duchess of York tried to give Elizabeth as relaxed an upbringing as possible under the circumstances, but when she was only nine months old they had to leave her in Buckingham Palace while they went on a long tour of Australia and New Zealand for the king. Royal duties interfered still more frequently after the duke himself became king when Elizabeth was ten years old, so the main responsibility for raising Elizabeth and later her sister Margaret fell to their nurse, Mrs. Clara Cooper Knight, and to their governess, Miss Marion Crawford.

Miss Crawford or "Crawfie," as she was called, wrote a book, *The Little Princesses,* about her experiences and, though always tactful and restrained in its opinions, it gives some insight into the childhood world of Elizabeth. Crawfie joined the household at the Royal Lodge in Windsor Park, a more informal royal residence than most. It was here that Elizabeth, who was five, had her Little House with its thatched roof and diamond-paned windows, a gift from the people of Wales. Inside were electric lights and workable plumbing, as well as complete sets of furniture, linen, and china. In the kitchen were canned goods, brooms, pots and pans—all in miniature—and on the bookshelves were children's books. Elizabeth and Margaret kept the house tidy and before going away they always stored the linens and blankets and wrapped the silver in newspapers so it would not tarnish, just as the servants did in the big house.

In the fall of 1933 the family moved to a town house at 145 Piccadilly in London. From the gardens behind it a gate opened into Hyde Park. The nurseries were attractive, light rooms on the top floor, and here Elizabeth kept her collection of toy horses on wheels. Each night before going to bed she carefully removed each saddle and groomed and watered each horse. Later when the family moved to Buckingham Palace the horses stood in a row in the corridor. They were still there on Elizabeth's wedding day. She always had her own ponies and horses and became an expert horsewoman. Once when Crawfie mentioned Elizabeth's obsession with horses to her father, he replied, "Think nothing of it. It is a family idiosyncrasy."

Lessons were given in a small cheerful room off the drawing room. At six Elizabeth could already read, for her mother had taught her. She was bright and quick to learn. Her first reading book was *Peter Pan in Kensington Gardens* by James M. Barrie, and she soon progressed to the *Children's Newspaper,* which gave simple explanations of the news. Her nurse had insisted she stay clean and had forbidden romps in the park, but Crawfie did her best to change this, and let Elizabeth get as dirty as she wished playing hide and seek in the bushes. Sometimes the duke joined the children for a game. People continually peered through the railings to catch a glimpse of the children, but although this made the governess very nervous, Elizabeth and Margaret did not seem to notice.

Miss Crawford wanted to show them something of life outside the garden and one day took them unobtrusively into Hyde Park where they went unnoticed. They stared with intense curiosity at other children but were not allowed to talk to them. Elizabeth longed to ride on the London subway, and it was arranged that she and Margaret could take a trip on it to visit the YWCA. The girls excitedly bought their own tickets and rode the escalator down to the train, a detective following at a discreet distance. At the YWCA no one paid much attention to them and Crawfie later wrote that "Tea out of thick cups, other people's bread and butter, tea you paid for with money, these were wonderful treats."

The duke and duchess tried to spend most evenings with their children. They seldom entertained, for the duke was not considered a very important member of the royal family. Far more attention was paid to his older brother, David, who was heir apparent. David often visited Elizabeth and Margaret and gave them a set of A. A. Milne's books. They memorized most of the poems in *When We Were Very Young*, and especially liked "Changing the Guard at Buckingham Palace."

At Christmas time the children bought their own family presents, usually from Woolworth's. They received many expensive gifts, but, according to their governess, the simple ones usually pleased them most. Their stockings were filled by their parents after they had fallen asleep.

The duke and duchess gave Miss Crawford a free hand with the children's education, and it was Queen Mary, the duke's mother, who took the greatest interest in their progress. She suggested that more time be devoted to history and Bible study and less to arithmetic, also that Elizabeth memorize more poetry, which she thought was "wonderful memory-training." Each morning after lessons there was a break for "elevenses," the morning snack, and often the duke came into the garden to play hopscotch with the children. There were also piano and singing lessons.

King George V was very fond of his grand-daughter Elizabeth, and she was not a bit intimidated by his gruff ways. "She was even at times a trifle patronizing," her governess wrote. "I remember on one occasion when he drew a rather crude picture for her, she stood at his elbow, watching, encouraging him. 'You really are not at all a bad drawer,' she said."

When he was ill she was sent to spend some time with him at the seashore, for her presence made him feel better.

Elizabeth studied French from an early age and became fluent in it. Later she also studied German, along with algebra, composition, literature, geography, and history. She had a temper but tried to control it and was generally reserved—a family trait—even as a child. "Schoolroom brawls often started when they had to wear hats," Miss Crawford wrote. "They hated hats. This put them in a bad humor, and they would snap one another's elastics to shrill cries of 'You brute!' 'You beast!' 'Margaret always wants what I want!' "

In 1936 the peaceful London life came to an end. Uncle David, who had succeeded to the throne as Edward VIII upon the death of his father, George V, abdicated to marry an American divorcee, Mrs. Wallis Simpson. Since the Church of England did not recognize divorce and no divorced person was even allowed entrance to the court, the romance shocked and dismayed the family. After David made his formal abdication speech, his brother, the shy duke of York, who had no desire for such a role, was named king as George VI. From that day on Elizabeth was required to curtsey to her father.

The family moved from the pleasant house in Piccadilly to Buckingham Palace, which they found huge, gloomy, and rather like "camping in a museum." It had been built in 1825, used by Queen Victoria, and enlarged by George V. The halls were heated, but the bedrooms had only fireplaces. Mice were everywhere. The rooms were so spread out that a postman had to deliver the mail between them and it took a day to walk from one end to the other. Now the children saw less of their parents, and it became harder and harder to protect them from photographers and publicity.

For her father's coronation in Westminster Abbey, Elizabeth wore a dress of lace and a cape trimmed with ermine. She and Margaret drove to the abbey in a carriage, waving to the crowds. Elizabeth, now eleven, took a protective attitude toward her sister, who was four years younger. "I do hope she won't disgrace us by falling asleep in the middle, Crawfie," she said anxiously. "After all, she is *very* young for a coronation, isn't she?" However, the long day passed without mishap, and the tired girls returned home, only to have to pose again and again for photographers.

Holidays were spent at Balmoral Castle in Scotland, which was very much as Queen Victoria had left it. There was tartan linoleum on the floors and tartan curtains in the windows. Dreary landscapes done by Queen Victoria's drawing teacher hung on the walls and a statue of Prince Albert stood in the front hall.

Tea was the high point of the day at Balmoral, with scones, hot sausage rolls, shrimps, and griddle cakes served in the drawing room. In the evening kilted pipers played their bagpipes while strolling through the house. Each year there was a ball for the "gillies," the outdoor male servants of the king. Elizabeth was permitted to dance some of the reels for the first time when she was twelve.

In an effort to introduce Elizabeth to children of her own age a troop of Girl Guides was started at the palace. Elizabeth was worried, though, because her sister was too young to join, and she pleaded with the Guide Commissioner, Miss Synge: "You don't think we could get her in somehow? . . . She is very strong, you know. Pull up your skirts, Margaret, and show Miss Synge. You can't say those aren't a very fine pair of hiking legs, Miss Synge. And she loves getting dirty, don't you, Margaret, and how she would love to cook sausages on sticks."

The problem was solved by making Margaret a Brownie. Later the palace had both Guide and Brownie troops made up of the children of the employees and of court officials. The king forbade their wearing what he called "those hideous long black stockings," for they reminded him of his boyhood.

Instead they wore tan knee socks, which all the Guides adopted later.

One weekend the family paid a visit to Dartmouth Royal Naval College, where the king had studied and where he was officiating at an inspection. Elizabeth, now thirteen, met a good-looking blond boy, Prince Philip of Greece, who was a student there. He and Elizabeth were third cousins, both great, great grandchildren of Queen Victoria. When the time came to leave, the cadets followed the royal yacht in their boats, rowing far out into the harbor. One boat was more persistent than the others. It was Philip's, and finally he had to be ordered back to the dock.

When World War II started, some of the king's advisers suggested that the children should be sent to a safer place, but the queen would have none of it. "The children could not go without me," she said simply, "and I could not possibly leave the king." They stayed at Windsor Castle throughout the hostilities.

During the first air raid, the shelter, which was in a dungeon, had not yet been properly equipped, and the princesses and the staff spent a gloomy, uncomfortable night while enemy aircraft flew overhead. Later a bedroom and bath were arranged for Elizabeth and her sister who, at the sound of the alarm, learned to dress quickly and rush for the shelter, each carrying a small suitcase of treasured belongings.

In 1940 Elizabeth made her first radio broadcast. She spoke to the children of the world who were separated from their families because of the war. Her words were very moving, and the listeners were especially touched by her spontaneous effort to include her sister at the end. "Come, Margaret, say good-night," she ordered. And then a small voice said, "Good-night, children."

Elizabeth was confirmed in the chapel at Windsor Castle in 1941. The service was simple and was nearly unnoticed because of the war. Little was ever said of what the future held for her, but she was aware of it and tried hard to do what was expected of her.

At sixteen she was made a colonel in the Grenadier Guards, which pleased her, for she knew many of the officers. As her duties increased, she was given a sitting room of her own. Up to this time she had always used the schoolroom and the nursery. Now she moved her books and some easy chairs into her own private quarters, and when she returned to Buckingham Palace after the war she had a suite of rooms to herself.

Philip, now a poised and handsome young man, came to Windsor Castle to visit, and from then on the two wrote to each other regularly. He was now a naval officer on board a ship in the Mediterranean. Elizabeth joined one of the women's services, the Auxiliary Territorial Service, where she learned how to take an engine apart and service a car. She was determined to keep up with her fellow trainees and worked hard for a year, when she was promoted. After passing the various driving tests, she drove through the London traffic to the palace, very proud of her achievement.

When the war ended, the princesses were allowed to join the joyous V-Day celebrations outside the gates of Buckingham Palace. Never before had royalty mixed with crowds of commoners, but the king let the two girls go with two officers and take part in the cheering.

Now Philip's little car parked outside the palace became a familiar sight. Everyone sensed that a romance was developing, and the newspapers published stories about the two young people, most of the information in them being inaccurate or untrue. Later Philip was invited to Balmoral to spend a month with Elizabeth, and people thought that surely an engagement would be announced. But at the end of the holiday no announcement was forthcoming and, although no one will ever know exactly what the king and queen really thought, it was guessed that they were unable to make up their minds about the suitability of the match. Philip, the son of the late Prince Andrew of Greece and Princess Alice of Battenberg, was a kind of royal waif. He had no private income and, though sixth in line to the Greek throne, had been raised in England by his uncle, Lord Louis Mountbatten, whose name he used. He had been educated at Cheam, a preparatory school in Surrey, and at Gordonstoun in Scotland prior to enrolling in the Naval College at Dartmouth. He had no Greek blood and looked and acted like a member of the British aristocracy, but he was not yet a British subject. The king and queen announced that they would take Elizabeth with them on a tour of South Africa. While away, she wrote to Philip frequently and kept his photograph on her dressing table.

At the end of the two-month tour, Elizabeth celebrated her twenty-first birthday in Capetown. For the occasion she broadcast a brief but poignant message, carried all over the world, in which she dedicated herself to the service of the empire.

After the return to London, King George at last gave his consent to the betrothal. Philip became a British citizen and renounced all claim to the throne of Greece. He was now plain Lieutenant Philip Mountbatten. He also formally gave up the Greek Orthodox Church, into which he had been born, and became a member of the Church of England. An independent, masculine, forthright person, who had knocked about the world a good deal and loved parties and fast sports cars, Philip undoubtedly thought long and hard about what changes in his life would be necessary as a prince consort. As soon as the engagement was announced a bodyguard from Scotland Yard was assigned to follow him everywhere. Philip was knighted by the king and given the title duke of Edinburgh.

The wedding, on November 20, 1947, was a welcome and colorful pageant for shabby, worn Londoners who were suffering through the lean postwar years. Thousands watched as Elizabeth rode from Buckingham Palace to Westminster Abbey, which had been filled hours earlier by diplomats, relatives, and friends. Precisely on schedule the aisle covering was rolled back and the gentlemen-at-arms in scarlet tunics and gold epaulettes marched to their places at the front of the church. Then officers of the Yeomen of the Guard in their red and gold full dress uniforms took up their stations in the nave. A glittering procession of royal guests entered, led by the queen and by Philip's mother. Dowager Queen Mary followed, erect despite her eighty years; then the visiting kings and queens, princes and princesses.

Philip and his best man, both in naval uniform, walked to the right of the altar and the dean of Westminster, who was to perform the service, took his place. As the drums rolled and the trumpets resounded through the abbey, Elizabeth, radiant in a white wedding gown and a diamond tiara, began her long walk down the aisle on the arm of her father. Two children, dressed in Royal Stuart kilts, carried her train.

At the close of the ceremony, the bells of St. Margaret's Church sounded jubilantly across London, and to the cheers of a half million onlookers the wedding party returned to Buckingham Palace for a wedding breakfast. There were many appearances on the balcony overlooking the Mall before the couple could leave for the town of Romsey and the nearby Mountbatten estate for their honeymoon. Even there they were besieged by crowds, and it was so difficult to find any privacy they finally drove to Scotland and Birkhall, the king's estate near Balmoral.

King George gave his daughter Clarence House on the Mall, not far from Buckingham Palace, and a twenty-five room house in Sunninghill Park near Ascot as her country home. Clarence House needed extensive repairs, as well as modern plumbing and central heating, so Elizabeth and Philip rented Windlesham Moor, a manor house in Berkshire, while the work was being done. The first months of marriage were difficult, even though Elizabeth had been freed from official duties until February. The work at Clarence House was demanding, and Philip was working full time at the Admiralty, as well as learning court etiquette, accompanying his wife to evening functions, and attending to his duties in the House of Lords. They began to spend nights in town at Kensington Palace and went less and less to Windlesham Moor. Just a year after their marriage a son was born to them in Buckingham Palace. He was christened Charles Philip Arthur George.

In May, 1949, the repairs to Clarence House, which seemed to have gone on endlessly, were finished, and Elizabeth and Philip at last had a home of their own. In October, however, Philip was sent to Malta as a first lieutenant on board a destroyer and, although Elizabeth flew there when she could, they were together only eight months in the next two years. Philip was soon given his first command, an antiaircraft frigate, but after a year he was recalled to what was described as "higher service," or what he sardonically dubbed "bazaar openings," and came reluctantly back to London.

A second child, Anne, had been born in August, 1950, and in the autumn of 1951 Elizabeth and Philip had to leave her and Charles once again for an extended tour of Canada and the United States. When Elizabeth stepped off the plane in Montreal, people suddenly noticed how much more attractive she had become. She was no longer overweight and her clothes were far more stylish than they had been at the time of her marriage. Her clothes were now less frilly and more flattering.

Hardly were she and Philip back from Canada when they left again for Australia and New Zealand. En route the royal party stopped in Kenya for an official visit and stayed in a hunting lodge which had been a wedding present from the people of Kenya. They also spent a night in a tree house from which they watched jungle animals come out of the bush to drink at a water hole. While Elizabeth was here, her father died unexpectedly in his sleep. Philip heard the news first, cabled London for confirmation, and then told his wife. Within hours they were airborne toward London where at a Privy Council meeting Elizabeth was named queen. She was twenty-five and the first woman to ascend the British throne in 115 years. Even before she could go to Sandringham to see her mother and Margaret, she had to attend to the "boxes," which from now on would follow her wherever she went, twice a day, seven days a week, as long as she reigned. In them are state papers, foreign dispatches, and confidential messages, many of which she must sign and all of which she has to read. She and Philip moved to Buckingham Palace, regretfully leaving behind the house they had spent so much time remodeling and barely lived in.

Elizabeth's coronation took place on June 2, 1953.

For days before, London was jammed with tourists. On the great day itself, traffic came to a standstill, and the only way to get about was by the subway. Three special trains were run to carry the nobility, accompanied by their pages, coronets in hand, to Westminster Abbey.

People had occupied places on the sidewalks lining the route many hours in advance. Armed with food, blankets, and pillows, they waited in the rain, good-humoredly singing "Tipperary" and "Waltzing Matilda." No discomfort was too great for a chance to see their queen.

During the long, solemn ceremony, marked by its medieval pomp, the archbishop of Canterbury placed the crown of Edward the Confessor on Elizabeth's head. Philip knelt before her to pledge his allegiance, as did all the dukes, earls, viscounts, and barons. After a brief silence the peers and peeresses of the realm put on their coronets, a gesture permitted only after the queen had been crowned, and the audience cried, "God Save Queen Elizabeth!" From the ancient Tower of London on the Thames River came the boom of guns. In a golden coach drawn by eight gray horses the queen later returned to Buckingham Palace, and from the balcony she acknowledged the greetings of her subjects. Charles and Anne were with her, tired after the strenuous day.

After Elizabeth became queen, some thought that
court life might become less formal, but this did not
happen. Instead she insisted that all traditions be
rigorously followed, including the one which forbade
divorced persons access to the court. Thus, her
uncle's wife, the duchess of Windsor, has never been
permitted a visit to the royal family, and Princess
Margaret, who fell in love with a divorced man,
Peter Townsend, was not allowed to marry him.

In the first ten years of her reign Elizabeth has
traveled more than four times around the world on
official visits. This is fatiguing work which constantly takes her away from her family. A second son,
Andrew, was born in 1960, not long after she had
returned from a grueling 15,000 mile trip across
Canada. As part of this tour, she and United States's
President Dwight D. Eisenhower dedicated the new
St. Lawrence Seaway at a ceremony in St. Lambert,
Quebec. The British newspapers at home com-
plained bitterly about the rigorous schedule the
Canadians had arranged for the queen. But regard-
less of how dull are the speeches she must listen to
or how weary she is of public appearances, Eliza-
beth never complains.

There is little about royalty's life that does not
come in for criticism at one time or another. The
people feel that the queen is public property, and
newspapers have written about everything from her

waistline to the happiness of her marriage. *The Daily Express,* a London tabloid owned by Lord Beaverbrook, has been particularly cruel, and once a Conservative member of Parliament protested what he called the newspaper's "personal vendetta" against the royal family, which by tradition is unable to defend itself. The queen is never allowed to discuss any controversial subject or express anything but the most general comments on public affairs.

Labor members of Parliament have presented a motion deploring the extravagances of the royal household. Princess Margaret's costly parties and clothes; the young man she married in 1960, a commoner named Antony Armstrong-Jones who to some seemed rather flamboyant and Bohemian; the expensive royal yacht—all have come in for their share of criticism. So far Queen Elizabeth has borne it with stoicism and poise.

A constant stream of important guests comes to pay respects to the queen. In June, 1961, President and Mrs. John F. Kennedy were entertained at a private dinner party in Buckingham Palace. And in July Yuri A. Gagarin, the Russian cosmonaut, lunched with Philip and the queen, talking enthusiastically through an interpreter.

The children see little of their parents. Charles was sent away to Cheam, the same school his father attended, when he was eight years old. From there he went to Gordonstoun. Philip, who is extremely keen about sports and was a fine cricket and polo player and yachtsman, is trying to encourage the same interests in his older son. Andrew, of course, is still too young for school or sports. Anne, like her mother, is devoted to horses and dogs. Both have had pet Corgis for as long as they can remember.

The queen's high sense of duty, her charm, and her handsome, appealing family endear her to her subjects, who are inevitably indignant when some-one asks why a monarchy which wields no political power and costs so much should thus endure. Elizabeth is a symbol of the unity which binds the Commonwealth countries together, and this seems to be reason enough for her role. Her guiding principle has been one of service, as she has struggled to keep her coronation vows: "I have in sincerity pledged myself to your service, as so many of you are pledged to mine. Throughout my life and with all my heart I shall strive to be worthy of your trust."

Index

Achillas, 14–16, 17–18
Akhetaten, city of, 1–12
Akhetaten (Amenhotep IV),
    king of Egypt, 1–12
Alaska, 121
Albert, prince consort of Vic-
    toria, 157, 160–163
Albret, Jeanne d', 62–63, 67
Alexander I, emperor of Rus-
    sia, 123
Alexander III (the Great),
    king of Macedon, 14
Alexandria, 14, 15–18, 23–25,
    27–28
Alexandrina, princess of Rus-
    sia, 123–124
Alexandrine War, 18
Alfonso, prince of Castile,
    43, 44
Alfonso V, king of Portugal,
    44, 48, 49
Amenhotep III, 3–4
Amenhotep IV (Akhetaten),
    1–12

America, colonization of, 54,
    78–79, 121
Andrew, prince of England,
    236, 238
Ankhsenpaaten, queen of
    Egypt, 11–12
Anne, princess of England,
    233, 235, 238
Antony, Mark, 13, 19–30, 33
Aragon, 42, 43, 45, 47, 49–
    50, 55
Armstrong-Jones, Antony,
    237
Arsinoë, 23
art, Egyptian, 8
Atenism, 5, 6–7, 11, 12
Augustus III of Poland, 120
Aurelian, 35–40
Austria, 119, 120, 127–128
    Maria Theresa of, 102–112
Austrian Succession, War of,
    105–108

Bacon, Francis, 76